£10

TAKE ME
TO YOUR
Leader

——————————— Rediscovering the Heart of ———————————
Spiritual Leadership

LES WHEELDON

ISBN:10: 151503996X
ISBN:13: 978-1515039969

DEDICATION

To all the leaders known and unknown,
who love and serve the Lord Jesus Christ.

Foreword

There are a myriad of books written on Christian leadership, many of which present ideas that can come across more theoretical than reality, lacking Biblical substance and integrity. It is therefore so refreshing to read Les's book *Take Me To Your Leader* which presents the key core value for Godly leadership, that being to firstly know the Lord intimately in order to effectively represent Him publicly.

Les's writings are presented as a genuine cry of the Holy Spirit for present day leaders to return back to their first love, and for any who may be aspiring to be a (future) leader in the Body of Christ, this book should be read, and reviewed on a regular basis.

John Elliott
Director, World Outreach International

ACKNOWLEDGMENTS

This book is not a treatise on leadership. It is much rather a collection of my reflections on the subject. My purpose is to challenge my readers to pray that God will continue to revive the spiritual life of Churches and so reveal His heart through His amazing family – the Church. I have included a chapter on the preaching ministry from the "The Christian's Compass" as I believe it is of particular relevance in this book. I am particularly grateful to many close friends including: Blaesius Fultang, Graham Cline, Tim Cross, Mary Seaton, Andrew Greener, Cathy Ellis, Matt Chilvers and Sandy Robertson for reading this book and encouraging me in this project. I am thankful to God for so many friends who rejoice to see what God is doing in this present generation. Finally I am greatly indebted to my wife Vicki for her tireless contribution in encouraging me and editing the manuscript.

Les Wheeldon

CONTENTS

The Emperor and the Heir

There was once a very old Chinese emperor who had no heir to succeed him. There was much consternation in the kingdom. Then one day the emperor invited any man who would like to succeed him, to come to the palace to undergo a trial to determine who would be the next ruler.

About 500 eager young men gathered and at last the emperor came out carrying a large tray of various seeds. He invited each one to take one seed and to return in six months with what he was able to produce from it. One man named Lee Wang, took a seed and hurried home with it. He did not know what kind of seed it was so he took a big pot and filled it with the best brown earth he could find, and carefully pressed the seed into a depth of about three inches. He watered it just enough to make it germinate, and waited for several days, but nothing appeared. After two weeks had passed he suspected that the seed he had picked was dead. He went to visit others who had taken a seed and saw to his horror that their seeds had indeed begun to sprout.

The six months passed slowly and Lee Wang had no desire to return to the palace but the emperor had made them promise that whatever they achieved, whether small or great, they would take it to display to the court. When Lee Wang arrived at the palace on the appointed day, his heart sank as he saw the flourishing shrubs and flowers that were on show.

The emperor came forth at the set hour and inspected each pot: he even paused at Lee Wang's empty pot where he seemed to linger thoughtfully. At last he announced that a successor had been found and to everyone's astonishment he pointed straight at Lee Wang. "You see," said the emperor, "When I gave you the seed six months ago, I baked the whole tray in a hot oven for three hours the day before I gave it to you." There were gasps of astonishment as everyone slowly realised that all who had brought shrubs and flowers were liars, and had substituted their dead seed for a living one. Only Lee Wang had told the truth. "You see," said the emperor, "we need a ruler who will not lie and pretend, but will live honestly before the people."

1

The meaning of the story is simple: Christian leadership should not be built on natural ambition but on humility and honesty of heart. Only if we have these qualities in us are we spiritually equipped to lead others.

REDISCOVERING THE HEART OF LEADERSHIP

Leadership is key to the vigour and strength of the local Church. Churches will vary in their leadership structure and will go through many adjustments as they mature in God. There are certainly many different aspects of leadership that can be changed through thoughtful attention to improving attitudes. It is right to address such issues as the art of delegation, how to motivate people to get involved etc.... But these are of minor significance and not to be compared with the heart of the matter.

The heart of leadership is spiritual and the purpose of leadership is to know God and to make Him known, which is God's ultimate blueprint for the Church itself. Just as Jesus was God's ultimate self-disclosure to the human race, so too the Church continues to be that self-disclosure as the body of Jesus Christ. It must be said reverently and with understanding, that the Church is the continuation of the incarnation. The Church is not God and will never be God, but she is the dwelling place of God through the presence of Christ by the Holy Spirit.

For this reason, this book is for every Christian who has a burden to see God's will and plan fulfilled in this current generation. All members of the Church, male and female, young and old, are urged to participate in this great calling to know Christ as our leader and to point people to Him. This book will not give "ten keys to Church growth" or "ten characteristics of a successful leader." It aims to encourage God's people to cultivate the attitude that enables God's plan to be fulfilled. The leaders of the Church have a critical role in this venture as examples to the flock in this great purpose of God.

Take me to your leader!

Imagine if a Martian heard that the God of the universe had created a people who could reveal His heart and nature. Imagine that this extra-terrestrial being then landed on planet earth and approached a Christian asking to be taken to his or her leader. Their answer should be to point to Christ, not to their pastor or elder.

God's desire is to have men and women on fire with a passion to introduce people to Himself, as the one who has the power, the wisdom and the skill to heal every life (not sure about Martians!). If leaders have this heart then the whole Church will be challenged to do the same.

Leadership is a journey - not an office or an administrative role. The road is long and will go through difficult valleys and magnificent mountain tops, but as we journey we will be increasingly conscious of the Great Shepherd who walks beside us as our companion and teacher. No matter how hard this journey may seem at times, it is not merely a journey in a forward direction, it is a passage from glory to glory.

PART I

~

THE SPIRITUAL LIFE OF LEADERS

"If Christians around the world were to suddenly renounce their personal agendas, their life goals and their aspirations, and begin responding in radical obedience to everything God showed them. the world would be turned upside down. How do we know? Because that's what first century Christians did, and the world is still talking about it."

— Henry T. Blackaby, Spiritual Leadership

CHAPTER 1

THE ENTHRONING OF CHRIST.

Christ the Leader of His Church.

Christ is the actual head of the Church – not the honorary figurehead. Truly spiritual leaders seek to actively enthrone Christ both in their personal lives and in every sphere where they hold influence and authority. Once that important fact is accepted, the leaders will take their rightful place among the people. If this is not understood, there will be an unconscious usurping of Christ's authority and not an establishment of it.

It may be objected that Jesus does not need our help to be enthroned as the Lord of all. He declared after His Resurrection that *"all authority has been given to Me in heaven and in earth."* (Matthew 28:18). This is true, and no one can alter this foundation of the universe that He is Lord of all and every knee will bow to Him. However, this rule of Christ is not to be merely acknowledged in a general manner, but in a personal and specific attitude of surrender to Him. In every heart there is a throne, and Christ must be welcomed and enthroned there.

This is true, not just of every individual, but of every home, every Church, every meeting, every business and every government. It was said of Ronald Reagan that he would kneel and pray for help in the decisions of government.

Thrones must be yielded to Him or His rule will not be known in the loving and personal touch that He alone brings.

When the King of Nineveh heard the preaching of Jonah:

> *"He arose from his throne and laid aside his robe, covered himself with sackcloth and sat in ashes."* Jonah 3:6.

He then used his authority to make a proclamation that the whole city should follow his lead and bow to the King of Kings.

Stage 1: Personal Surrender.

The first stage of enthroning Christ is in an act of entire surrender. By this Christ is enthroned as Lord of our lives. Often when Christians think of Christ's Lordship they think of a system of authority going back through the deacons, elders and pastors reaching ultimately to the person of Christ. This is how governments rule. How utterly different is the rule desired by God. In the UK taxpayers will receive a letter from the Inland Revenue with an emblem stating "On Her Majesty's service." This indicates that ultimately these officials are acting on behalf of the Head of State, the Queen. Very few taxpayers will ever actually meet her majesty, and very few are happy at the thought that they are supporting her Royal Highness financially! When the Queen, her prime minister and other government officials meet the public it is unheard of that any one falls prostrate surrendering all their money to them, and offering all up to the tax system. Most citizens are more often concerned to influence the government to reduce taxation, not increase it! Most importantly of all, no one bows and surrenders their inner self to the Queen or her ministers.

In contrast the Kingdom of God functions on the direct rule of Christ in the hearts of His people. Christians may be strongly encouraged to part with their money, giving sacrificially of their substance. But Christ is not satisfied with offerings of mere possessions and wealth. He wants the hearts of His people. True leadership begins here and springs from the heart of a person who has personally and directly touched the feet of Jesus, and known the Kingdom of God established in the inner sanctuary of the heart.

This is not as common an experience as may be assumed. In salvation the authority of Christ is experienced. When we repent and believe we are accepted into His kingdom, and have all the rights associated with this transfer of our citizenship. However the surrender of the inner sanctuary of the heart is a much deeper transaction. It will involve the willingness to let go of everything in order to know His loving rule. The result will be an immediate change in the note of the life. There will be a deeper peace, and an inner cessation of striving. Worry will vanish from the mind as the realization begins to take hold that Christ is Lord of all our circumstances, and that under Him we are secure. It does not mean that Christians are not secure until we surrender all, but it certainly means we need to surrender consciously to Him to experience the full wonder of the safety and security that are ours.

Many Christians will be baptized with the Holy Spirit at this point of entire surrender, while others will discover this to be the place of continuous infilling of the Holy Spirit. Many will experience a renewed sense of belonging entirely to Him and know a deeper work of the Holy Spirit each time they return to this Holy ground. Why is it Holy ground? Simply because it is all part of the great transaction of Calvary. Christ offered Himself to God in absolute surrender, and the same Holy Spirit works in us to produce the same attitude of heart.

"Christ, through the eternal Spirit offered Himself without spot to God." Hebrews 9:14.

This deeper work of the Holy Spirit releases us from our own plans and desires and is the basis of moulding us into one body:

"For by one Spirit we were all baptized into one body-whether Jews or Greeks, whether slaves or free-and have all been made to drink into one Spirit." 1 Corinthians 12:13.

The force of this verse is that in the baptism with the Holy Spirit there is an elimination of the things that commonly divide human beings. There is racial unity, and harmony between rich and poor. It is the fulfilment of the prophecy in Isaiah that *"the lion shall lie down with the lamb"* and not eat it! This is a miraculous state of peace founded upon the death of self-centred living.

The Kingdom of God is manifest in a Church when all the members are laying their lives, their preferences, their careers, their whole life on the altar.

The place of surrender is spiritual, but it is also practical. As John said:

"He who does not love his brother whom he has seen, how can he love God whom he has not seen?" 1 John 4:20.

Submission to God will produce mutual submission among God's people in general and among His ministers in particular. This is a place of safety and protection, that as we learn to be submitted one to another, we are correctable and accountable. This will itself protect leaders from many of the pitfalls of human leadership.

Stage 2: **Waiting on God.**

Waiting on God is the most important attitude of leaders, since it is in and through this relationship with Him that His rule is maintained and applied to our lives and sphere of influence. The most common mistake in this respect is to believe that this is waiting **for** God rather than waiting **on** God. The servants who waited on King Solomon were not waiting for him to show up! They were actively attentive to His every need. They did this with such joy and zeal that the Queen of Sheba was overwhelmed by the attitude of the King's servants:

> *"And when the Queen of Sheba had seen the wisdom of Solomon, the house that he had built, the food on his table, the seating of his servants, the service of the waiters and their apparel, his cupbearers and their apparel, and his entryway by which he went up to the house of the Lord, there was no more spirit in her."* 2 Chronicles 9:3-4.

Waiting on God is for those who are continually taking up their ministry to the King. Ministering to Him is the foundation of all ministry. Churches exist to satisfy the heart of Jesus, to exalt Him, to know Him and to make Him known. The clothing of Solomon's servants is specifically mentioned, and those who wait on Him will be clothed with dignity and the touch of His glory reflected in their faces, whether they wear jeans or business suits!

How then do we enter into this ministry of waiting on God? The answer is that we are to find the place where all inner noise has been stilled. The enemy of His leadership in the Church is the clamour of our hearts. Inner noise does not vibrate the ear drum, it disturbs and distracts the heart. Inner noise is produced by lusts and desires that draw the concentration away from God. The attitude of the Holy Spirit is one of total rapt concentration on Jesus, and nothing has ever distracted this focus. This is in effect the atmosphere of heaven, where angels gaze on God to minister to Him, and to do His will.

Concentration on Jesus is the attitude of waiting on God. It is not achieved merely by hours of contemplative prayer, but rather by a turning away from lesser things that are not worthy of the soul. Concentrating on Jesus is not through mental strain, but through the directing of the soul. Just as a telescope can be focused on a star, so the soul needs to position itself and then focus on God. The result will be the inner connection to God, and in this attitude we serve God. His authority clothes us there and we are endued with an authority that is not from our strength of personality, but from the absolute and infinite authority of Christ Himself.

The key then is to turn from ourselves in self-denial, and cultivate a quiet, listening heart. Hearing God is the chief faculty of all leaders. This is an intimidating thought, because we are often shy of claiming to have heard the voice of God. The truth is that many Christians especially in the West are far too unfamiliar with spiritual life. Christians often mistake their power of intellect for the Holy Spirit. In fact, He imparts knowledge to the heart which then dawns like a sunrise. We should not wait on God for "words" or prophecies. This often leads to frustration and disappointment. We should direct our hearts to God and let the Holy Spirit bathe us in His love and purity. As we wait there we will become aware of things that distil on our conscious mind. We become aware of unseen things such as the glory of Christ. By waiting on God the inner faculty of perceiving God and His will is sharpened.

This is the faculty that Jesus spoke of when He taught the disciples about the gift of the Holy Spirit. He taught them that by this gift they would know the wonder of indwelling:

> *"At that day you shall know that I am in my Father, and you in Me and I in you." (John 14:20)*

John speaks of the inner anointing by which we know all things (1 John 2:27). This is the knowledge of things that cannot be known by any other means. Just as we learn to read through teachers at school, so we know God's love and presence in us by the anointing. No book can teach us this, only as we listen to the voice of the Spirit in the heart do we learn this. The voice of the Holy Spirit is the voice of a dove and is itself quiet and brings calm. Every human being longs for this quiet place of rest, where all worry and striving cease and we know that we have truly come home. This place is the centre of the Christian's joy because it liberates us from selfishness. The presence of Jesus is so majestic and beautiful, that whoever gazes on Him forgets everything else, and is lost in worship of that matchless One.

When we truly wait on God something happens deep in the soul that is indescribable and yet affects everything we do. In the soul that waits on God there comes a fragrance that is the knowledge of Jesus. This is not merely spiritual indulgence, because the sight of Jesus to the eye of the soul delivers us from the smallness of self-seeking. Gazing on Jesus we become conscious of His greatness. Other things fade away, and most of all our own importance. We become incidental and all we want is to be allowed to be there and behold Him. Jesus is Himself the very definition of beauty, and there is no greater joy than to be aware of Him. To touch the hem of His garment is to be healed, and to be conscious of His inner life is to be transformed. Eternal life is not only endless existence, it is to be joined forever to this fathomless fountain of love and purity. There are things that are taught and things that are caught. We may be taught the facts about Jesus but it is when we linger in His presence that we catch the majesty, the rest, the peace that adorn Him. When leaders have been with Jesus, there are elements to their ministry that awaken thirst to know Him. There are things communicated unconsciously and it is these things that make us ministers of His Spirit, rather than merely ministers of truths about Him.

Stage 3: Lingering longer.

> *"And the people waited for Zacharias, and marvelled that he lingered so long in the temple." (Luke 1:21)*

There is a moment that is given to all who seek the face of God, when we have drunk deeply of the waters of life. Our deepest thirst has been satisfied, and we are at rest in the arms of God. This is the calm that is the antechamber to discovering God for Himself. Many Christians at this point simply have received all that they ever wanted and get on with their life. They remember this mountain top and refer back to it. But there are some who are not yet satisfied, and sense that they have only tasted, and that there is an ocean of living water yet to be discovered. This is the passion of the apostle Paul in Philippians 3:7-15:

> *"But what things were gain to me, these I have counted loss for Christ. Yet indeed I also count all things loss for the excellence of the knowledge of Christ Jesus my Lord, for whom I have suffered the loss of all things, and count them as rubbish, that I may gain Christ and be found in Him, not having my own righteousness, which is from the law, but that which is through faith in Christ, the righteousness which is from God by faith; that I may know Him and the power of His resurrection, and the fellowship of His sufferings, being conformed to His death, if, by any means, I may attain to the resurrection from the dead.*
> *Not that I have already attained, or am already perfected; but I press on, that I may lay hold of that for which Christ Jesus has also laid hold of me. Brethren, I do not count myself to have apprehended; but one thing I do, forgetting those things which are behind and reaching forward to those things which are ahead, I press toward the goal for the prize of the upward call of God in Christ Jesus. Therefore let us, as many as are mature, have this mind; and if in anything you think otherwise, God will reveal even this to you."*

These words are the passionate appeal of every true leader. Paul is not captivated by his ministry, or by works of power, or by success. He is enthralled with the knowledge of Jesus Christ, and he has let go of everything to discover this.

It is vital to be convinced of this, that the greatest need in all the world is for the knowledge of God. There are experts in preaching, Greek, Hebrew, Theology etc. but none of these can of themselves give life. The passion of a leader is to lead others to drink of the eternal fountains of living water from which he himself is constantly drinking. The world is perishing from the lack of the knowledge of God. While it would be wrong to measure our leadership by the hours we spend in prayer, it is nevertheless true that our leadership is measured by the depth to which we identify with Paul's passion for God Himself. If we truly know how to find that Presence then nothing else will satisfy.

The young seeker after God turns his face upwards to God in prayer. But the leader who has to minister to others, turns his face to the people. The danger is then that the leader turns more to the people than to God. The result is dryness of soul and a loss of the consuming passion that can motivate others to go deeper with God. Leadership that has lost this quality will ultimately decline into mere administration and fall back into usurping the leadership of God.

> *"If a man dethrone God he always makes himself God. If God does not occupy the throne of every life then man will assume for Himself the very functions of Deity." (G. Campbell Morgan, Acts of the Apostles, p. 233)*

Such a person may not even wait for God, let alone wait on God. Paul was a true leader because his heart was not drawn into the snare of serving people as a substitute for knowing God.

Serving God is not contradictory to serving people. The Christian disciple is a strange mixture of going deep and going out. Most think that it is a choice between a quiet life of contemplation, or a life of service. We are either Martha or Mary. Christianity does not exalt solitude, but rather sees it as the foundation for community. If a Church has no leaders who know the quiet place of fellowship with God, it will be a waterless wasteland. Equally those who follow God for selfish indulgence in quietness will find barrenness of soul.

The apostle Paul exhibits the poise of a man in touch with God but in the thick of activity for the souls of men. It is astonishing that Paul even worked with his hands to support himself and his team. Should such a man of prayer waste his time making tents? The answer is that prayer shapes the soul for life. If we pursue prayer for its own end then we develop an imbalanced soul which will be ultimately of no use to God or man. The person who prays will go out to seek the lost, and the person who goes out to seek the lost will often be on his knees praying.

Stage 4: Avoiding the Idolatry of Prayer.

God is the Creator of the human soul. He understands us so perfectly and leads us with consummate wisdom. The Quakers led by George Fox began to meet regularly in silent waiting on God, waiting for the Holy Spirit to speak. After some time the Quakers began to worship the silence rather than God. They swapped the living God for the idolatry of silence. Christians who find God will discover that God does not allow them to control their relationship with Him by following methods.

This is the experience of all who love Christ for Himself, that they pass through periods when all their methods stop working. Mary and Joseph took Jesus to the Passover when He was twelve years old, and on the way back to Nazareth they assumed that Jesus was somewhere in the crowd of friends and relatives. They assumed He would be where He always was, but to their consternation He was not to be found. They had to retrace their steps and seek Him. It is amazing that it took them three days to find Him (Luke 2:41-50). There were aspects to their little boy that now astonished and amazed them. So it must be in our seeking of God.

In the Song of Solomon there are two occasions when the Shulamite bride of Solomon cannot find Him. On the first occasion she finds him quickly (Song of Solomon 3:1-4) but on the second occasion she is hindered and suffers wounds in the process of her seeking (Song of Solomon 5:6-8). The process of overcoming the obstacles leads her to deeper love for Solomon, the chief of ten thousand (Song of Solomon 5:10). It is when God withdraws Himself for a season that our souls are purged from mere religious habits of prayer. So many have a "quiet time" without knowing His presence. God watches over His people to stir them to seek Him and to know Him for Himself.

Conclusion: Christ must be enthroned in our hearts through surrender and prayerful attention to His rule in our lives. The leader who does not know Christ closely may be a good leader in human terms but his leadership will fall short of the will of God, which is to connect every believer with God Himself through His Son Jesus Christ.

CHAPTER 2

THE CALL OF MOSES

The life of Moses has had a huge impact on world history. He would have been shocked before he reached the age of 80 to think that after 3,500 years people would be studying his life and reading the words he wrote. He was up to that point a nobody, a shepherd, without hope of political influence living in the deserts of present day Saudi Arabia. The aim of this chapter is to examine the call of Moses and the events which led up to the great turning point in his life at the burning bush.

Moses was a servant leader, willing even to be blotted out of the book of life to obtain mercy and forgiveness for the nation. The word "leader" occurs many times in the Bible, but the word "servant" occurs probably twice as often, which indicates the kind of leader God requires among His people. Jesus Himself is the greatest example of a servant leader, washing the disciples' feet and giving His life as a ransom for the sins of the world (Mark 10:45).

Leadership is a key for the flourishing of the work of God, and it is His plan to raise up leaders, both men and women, who will act in accordance with God's heart. Jesus lamented that Israel was scattered as sheep without a shepherd (Matthew 9:36-37). He continued by exhorting his disciples to pray for labourers to be sent into the harvest. Israel had leaders in the time of Christ but they were not leading the nation according to God's heart, but to fulfil their own selfish agenda. The life of Moses has much to teach us.

The call of God

Moses was called. This simple fact has a parallel in every believer's life. All God's people are called and are to understand the implications of this fact. The calling is expressed in Mark 3:13-15:

> *"And He went up on the mountain and called to Him those He Himself wanted. And they came to Him. Then He appointed twelve, that they might be with Him and that He might send them out to preach, and to have power to heal sicknesses and to cast out demons."*

The call was primarily "to be with Him," and can be defined as an inner sense of destiny, of purpose both for this life and beyond it. The call is a longing, a quest, an urge to fulfil the purpose for which we were created. There are facets to human life that lie completely dormant until awakened by the call. It is for this reason that human beings can easily occupy themselves with trivial superficial pastimes until they are arrested by the call of God. Once that inner voice is heard there will be disquiet until we have brought our lives into line with God's person and will for our lives. The call is to know Him, to partner in life with Him.

> *"Well do I remember,"* said Hudson Taylor, *"how I poured out my soul before God. Again and again confessing my grateful love to Him who had done everything for me ... I besought Him to give me some work to do for Him as an outlet for love and gratitude ... Well do I remember as I put myself, my life, my all upon the altar, the deep solemnity that came over my soul with the assurance that my offer was accepted ... A deep consciousness that I was not my own took possession of me."* Having made the great surrender, he was ready to hear the voice of his Lord saying, *"Who will go for Me to China?"* and to reply, *"Here am I, send me."*
>
> J. Hudson Taylor: God's Mighty Man of Prayer

Moses and Jesus have many parallels:

Moses	Christ
Moses was born and immediately set in the River Nile after which he was free from slavery	Christ was born of the Spirit and was not under the slavery of sin.
Moses was tempted in the wilderness 40 years before he began his ministry	Jesus was tempted 40 days in the wilderness before starting his ministry
Moses went up the mountain to give the Law. The ten commandments were given to control outward behaviour and convict of inward sin.	Jesus gave the sermon on the mount (Matt. 5) - the key teaching of the New Testament. Jesus promised inner renewal and the power to keep us from within.
Moses' face shone with the glory (Exod. 34:35)	The face of Jesus shone at the transfiguration (Mark 9:1)
Moses prayed that He would be cut off from God for the forgiveness of the people, but his prayer was not accepted	Jesus was accepted as a sacrifice for the sins of the people.
After the death of the lamb at Passover Moses built the tabernacle	Jesus after his death as the Lamb of God at Passover He built the Church.
Moses died by faith, not of natural causes on Mount Nebo (Deut 34:5-7)	Jesus died by faith committing His spirit into the hands of God (John 10:17-18; Luke 23:46)

****

Moses' time line

BC 1526	Birth of Moses Exodus 2. Hidden in the bulrushes by his parents, he is rescued and adopted by an Egyptian princess. He was brought up in the palace in a life of privilege.
BC 1486	Moses attempts to free the people by his own hand (Exodus 2; Acts 7:23), aged 40.
BC 1470?	Moses composes Psalm 90 possibly before his 70th birthday (see verse 10.)
BC 1446	Moses sees the Lord in the burning bush and is sent back to Egypt (Exodus 3, Acts 7:30) aged 80.
BC 1446-44	The people are delivered from Egypt and prepare to enter the land, they build the tabernacle, but rebel and are refused entry. (Numbers 14:22-3).
BC 1408	Moses is angered by the rebels and strikes the rock twice and is refused entry to the promised land (Numbers 20).
BC 1407	Moses gives the law the second time and recounts the history of the deliverance of Israel (book of Deuteronomy).
BC 1406	Moses dies by faith at the age of 120: (Deut 34:7).

****

1. The call of Moses: the faith of his parents

Hebrews 11.23 tells us of his parents' faith:

"By faith Moses, when he was born, was hidden three months by his parents, because they saw he was a beautiful child; and they were not afraid of the king's command." (Hebrews 11:23)

They risked all to save their son from death, because they saw that he was a beautiful child. This was the eye of faith. If parents look critically on their child, or a pastor looks negatively on a Church member, they may see with the eye of flesh and be critical. But the eye of faith sees beauty and potential.

God is looking for something far greater than our perceived usefulness to Him in this life. God sees us as perfect in Christ, and our worship to Him is the greatest fragrance. He does not see our worship just as singing songs in a Church meeting! He sees our lives in the glorious setting of eternity. He sees us as we will be after His grace has perfected us. This is how we must love and esteem our family, friends and fellow pilgrims. An orchid springs from a wrinkled ugly tuber. It has no beauty until a touch of moisture awakens the process of flowering. God's spirit touches the deepest potential of our human personality and awakens the beauty within. Blessed is the woman or man who has spiritual parents and faithful friends who see the beauty and not the faults.

The impact of believing parents can also be seen in the life of Samson. His calling began when God appeared to his mother (Judges 13:3-5). She was given prophetic insight into her son's future and was called to separate herself to the Lord through a Nazirite vow. The implication was that if she did not devote herself to the Lord, then her son Samson would never have the opportunity to fulfil his own calling. Her faith impacted her son. The same can be seen in the life of John the Baptist and Zachariah and Elizabeth as they served the Lord and walked in righteousness (Luke 1:6). Timothy was impacted by the faith of his mother and grandmother (2 Timothy 1:5). Proverbs 31 are the words of King Lemuel who learned wisdom from his mother (Proverbs 31:1). The impact of a life lived for God can never be measured. Monica, the mother of Augustine and Susannah the mother of John and Charles Wesley could never have guessed that their faith and prayers would impact so many through their children.

This does not mean that those without godly parents are at a disadvantage. It means that the work of God is a river with many tributaries as His children live for Him and serve Him.

2. Moses in Pharaoh's palace.

Moses was educated in all the culture and learning of the Egyptians. He had a life of privilege as the step-son of Pharaoh's daughter (possibly the Hatshepsut who ruled Egypt as regent in the reign of Thutmose III. Some speculate that Hatshepsut was a young princess of 15 when she adopted Moses). Moses would have had a first class education, and also enjoyed a privileged life-style with luxurious food and expensive clothing. Most importantly, he did not feel the lash of the overseer's whip.

3. The repentance of Moses.

At some point Moses realized he belonged to the oppressed people of God, who were slaves in Egypt. There were five aspects to his profound change of heart:

- He refused to be called the son of Pharaoh's daughter (Hebrews 11:24)
- He chose to suffer affliction (Hebrews 11:25)
- He esteemed the reproach of Christ greater riches (Hebrews 11:26)
- He forsook Egypt (Hebrews 11:27)

- All these things he did by faith (Hebrews 11:24-27)

Moses' repentance required faith. He forsook Egypt - including the privileged position and life-style he had enjoyed all his life until his fortieth year. It is easy to forget that so much of our spiritual power ultimately depends on the depth of our repentance. Repentance is the first essential response to the call of God. It is an awareness of the shallowness and emptiness of this world and its pleasures. Moses knew that there was something greater than his life of privilege in the palace of Pharaoh. So too, true repentance is a turning away from the hollowness of existence without God.

Humanity was created for something greater than mere subsistence or shallow pleasures. People may have amusement through multi-media, through food and drink, possessions and riches, and yet sense a dreadful emptiness and futility. Humanity was created for something greater, and that greater thing is the knowledge of God and the experience of His presence.

4. Moses tried to 'help' in his own strength.

"Now it came to pass in those days, when Moses was grown, that he went out to his brethren and looked at their burdens. And he saw an Egyptian beating a Hebrew, one of his brethren. So he looked this way and that way, and when he saw no one, he killed the Egyptian and hid him in the sand." (Exodus 2:11-12)

Little information is given about Moses' motive in killing the Egyptian. He may have believed that this was the beginning of a movement that would free the nation. Like Peter and other great men of God, he possibly believed in himself, his power, intelligence and strength of will. But he suffered the humiliation of his own failure and had to flee (Exodus 2:13-15).

Billy Graham and the Botswanan pastor

Ruth and I sat down and shook his hand. From his clothes we suspected that he came from a poor country and had very little. But his face had a gentleness and a joy about it that were immediately apparent.

"Where are you from?" I enquired.

"I am from Botswana."

In response to my gentle prodding, he told us something about his ministry. He said he travelled, often on foot, from village to village, preaching the gospel of Christ to anyone who would listen. It was he admitted, discouraging at times, with frequent opposition and very little response.

"Are there many Christians in Botswana?" I asked.

"A few," he replied. "Only a very few."

"What is your background? Did you go to Bible school or get any education to help you?"

"Well actually," he said, "I got my master's degree from Cambridge university."

'Just as I am' by Billy Graham, pp 557-8

****

"There must be great renunciations if there are to be great Christian careers."
James Denny

****

5. Moses' wilderness years.

Moses spent forty long years in the Arabian desert. As time rolled by he must have believed that if deliverance ever came for his people, it would be through another. The whole point of the wilderness is that there is nothing there. Moses was not on the path of wealth and fame. His life was now that of a common labourer and it was drawing to its natural end. During this time, Moses entered into a deep stillness of soul, quietly waiting on God. This is the mark of God's prophets, equipping them for deep face-to-face encounters with God and an ability to hear from Him. This stillness of soul is one of the most beautiful qualities of a minister; providing the Churches with much needed prophetic utterance and insight.

Later in Deuteronomy chapters 6-8 Moses taught the people about the lessons they had learned in their 40 years of wandering in the wilderness, which were probably the lessons he had first learnt alone. Jesus quotes from this section of Deuteronomy when resisting the three temptations in His wilderness experience.

Temptation 1:

"So He humbled you, allowed you to hunger, and fed you with manna which you did not know nor did your fathers know, that He might make you know that man shall not live by bread alone; but man lives by every word that proceeds from the mouth of the LORD." (Deut 8:3; c.f. Matthew 4:4)

Moses learned that the prime need of every person is to hear the word of God. To receive this word, the human heart must be deeply humbled and weaned from other tastes and appetites, so that this deepest thirst of all may possess us.

Temptation 2:

"You shall not tempt the LORD your God as you tempted Him in Massah." (Deut 6:16; c.f. Matthew 4:7)

Jesus quoted this when He was tempted to do an impressive miracle. His answer reveals that it is wrong to tempt God by "forcing" Him to do a miracle. Moreover, this was a temptation to behave like a circus performer dazzling a crowd with his skills. This temptation may be presented to us by Satan to turn the Church into a place to merely entertain or impress the world. This would be to tempt God and not to trust Him.

Temptation 3:

"You shall fear the LORD your God and serve Him, and shall take oaths in His name." "You shall worship the LORD your God, and Him only you shall serve." (Deut 6:13; c.f. Matthew 4:10)

Our primary purpose is to worship God. It is as we worship God alone that our lives are re-set. Clocks lose time and need re-setting when they become inaccurate. Our minds and hearts lose their focus and need to be re-calibrated. This can only happen as we approach God in worship. As we worship we are strengthened to overcome temptation.

6. God called him out of the burning bush (Exodus 3:2).

The bush is a symbol of a person's life burning for God, but without human intensity. The bush remained green and was not consumed. So the life that is full of the Holy Spirit is not driven by human passion and will, but by the divine presence in the soul of man. Moses was ready to see this vision because he was no longer trusting in his own power to deliver the people. The greatest example of a life burning for God is Jesus Himself. There was no strain or striving in His total devotion but rather poise and rest.

Just as Moses turned aside to see this great sight, so too the first steps in our knowledge of the call come when we meet someone who is walking with God. We often meet people who are genuinely God-fearing, and zealous about the Bible and the existence of God. But it is arresting and life-changing to meet a person walking closely with God.

The work of God is often accomplished unconsciously in the one whom God uses. There are things that are taught in sermons and Bible classes but there are also things that are "caught." One may teach about the love of God, but it is another thing to unconsciously convey our love for God and His word. There are things that can only be taught and things that can only be caught.

The disciples walking with Jesus caught the sense of the eternal, of His love for the Father and of His deep rest in the love of the Father. Moses "turned aside" to see "this great sight" and this reflects his thirst for God. When the sense of destiny is dulled and dead in the heart, then there is little response when the Holy Spirit moves. We must guard our hearts to keep them in healthy hunger for the things of God.

7. The call is given.

God clearly explained to Moses that He had heard the cry of the oppressed people of Israel and that He had appeared to Moses to send him to set the people free.

One may imagine that a much younger Moses would have jumped to attention and declared "I'm your man." God's appearance to Moses was supernatural and the promise God was making was electrifying. Normally such words would fill a soul with wonder and inspiration. But Moses was not only humbled by his experiences, he was deeply apprehensive and not ready to respond.

Moses resisted God's call with five excuses:

i.   With commendable humility.

"Who am I?" (Exodus 3:11). Moses' first step of resisting the call of God must have pleased God. Moses did not respond with bravado or self-confidence. He responded with deep humility aware that he did not have the answer to the problems of his people.

God's answer was to assure Moses that He would be with him and that He would be the means of setting the people free. (Exodus 3:12). Though it is the simplest truth, it is at the same time the most comforting, and is the very name of Jesus: Immanuel – God with us.

> *John Wesley died on March 2, 1791, in his eighty-eighth year. As he lay dying, his friends gathered around him, Wesley grasped their hands and said repeatedly, "Farewell, farewell." At the end, summoning his remaining strength, he cried out, "The best of all is, God is with us," lifted his arms and raised his feeble voice again, repeating the words, "The best of all is, God is with us."*

That God is with us may be the simplest truth, but it is profound and is amplified by the words of Romans 8:31: *"If God be for us, who can be against us?"* God is with us in all His love and power to protect and bless. When a person walks in the will of God they can be confident that all the power and resources of God are with them and all the armies of heaven are protecting them.

ii.   Moses did not know God's name.

Moses second question is also commendable.   He essentially confessed he did not know God.

"Who are you?" (Exodus 3:13) he said.

God's answer was to declare to Moses His majestic name "Yahweh." God said that the people did not know Him by this name (Exodus 6:3). This did not mean that they had never heard of this name, for it is found throughout the book of Genesis and is found throughout the account of God's dealings with Abraham. (E.g. Genesis 15:6 *"And he believed in the LORD (Yahweh), and He accounted it to him for righteousness.")* Abraham knew the name but God was going to reveal its full meaning to Moses.

There are two key implications from this name "I AM." First God is God of the present, not the future. The Hebrew tense is ambiguous and can be translated "the one who was, is, and shall be." However the New Testament is not ambiguous and refers to the one who is in the present: *"Before Abraham was, I am." (John 8:58).* God is not separated from us by time. He is not in the distant future, nor in the misty past, He is the God of the present. Unbelief can imagine miracles in the past or the future but not the present. God declares that He is the God of now.

The second meaning of "I AM" is one of the most important lessons for the Christian. God did not say "I do" though it would be true to say that He is the God of great deeds ... from creation ... to the parting of Red Sea ... to the raising of Lazarus. But God cannot "do" something in the human heart that sets us free from sin, He can only "be" that by His presence.

> *Once I was visiting Siberia, holding meetings in Churches and preaching in a Bible school, when I was gripped a with terrible toothache! My friends immediately arranged for me to see the local dentist, who proved to be a very large Russian with enormous fingers. He set to work with amazing dexterity and skill quickly solving my problem. I thanked him, paid the bill and left.*
> *I have never needed to see him again I am glad to say, as my problem was solved .*

A dentist can do great work on our teeth, and we will visit one when the need arises, but we do not expect that dentist to become a 'presence' in our lives. We should not treat God as a person to go to only when we have an emergency. God does not want to just 'do' something in our soul that will make us spiritual; He wants to achieve this through His Presence abiding in us and by a constant relationship with Him. If the relationship is lost, the spiritual power evaporates. It is for this reason that a believer may have a clear experience of new birth, but can still fall into sin by neglecting the power of their new life which is 'Christ in us.'

In the unfolding story of the redemption of the people from Egypt, God was to be with His people. It was God Himself who stood over the door stained with the lamb's blood and it was He who kept the destroyer out (Exodus 12:23). It was God who stood in the pillar of fire and cloud in the midst of the Red Sea to block the path of

Pharaoh (Exodus 14:24). It was God who declared His plan to come and live in a tent among the people (Exodus 25:8). Israel was saved by God's direct presence in the centre of the nation.

iii.   **A bad case of low self-esteem.** *"They will not listen to me!" (Exodus 4:1).*

Moses was not being humble in this objection, he was displaying the common human affliction of a very low self-worth. Moses had gone through many bitter experiences and these had produced a sense of being of no value to God or man.

God's answer was to challenge Moses by asking *"What is in your hand?"* Moses held his shepherd's staff in his hand, and threw it to the ground as God instructed him. The rod symbolized Moses former life. It bore scars of earlier conflicts and may even have been blood stained from defending the sheep against wolves. The rod was dead and barren and became a snake to threaten Moses. Our past experiences may be very complex. Moses grew up far from his natural parents, and probably in a hostile emotionally complex environment. It is often easy to forget how complicated we are through things that have happened to us as well as things that we have done. All human beings are subjected to abuse of various kinds, and it is vital to understand how God can heal the deep hurts of our hearts.

Moses was able to conquer this darkness by throwing the whole matter before God. Our past may threaten us like a serpent, but Moses is told to lay hold of the snake. He seized it by the tail and it became a rod of power in God's hand. God is able to heal the deepest wounds that have afflicted us, and then is able to use our evidence of a healed life to share this restoring power with others who are also in need of healing. Moses had thrown away the old broken life and found his life new, healed and full of the power of Yahweh.

iv.   A lame excuse!

Moses fourth objection was his speech defect (Exodus 4:10). Moses may have had a stammer or some other impediment. He felt totally unqualified for the task God was giving him. God's answer was to remind Moses, that He had created human beings and allowed them to be born with their various handicaps and weaknesses. The point is that God uses unqualified people so that all the glory goes to Him. Paul discovered that the weaker he was the more God's power rested on him:

> *"And He said to me, "My grace is sufficient for you, for My strength is made perfect in weakness." Therefore most gladly I will rather boast in my infirmities, that the power of Christ may rest upon me." (2 Corinthians 12:8)*

v.   Transparent honesty at last!

At last Moses admits the truth, digs his heels in and implores *"Please send someone else!"* (Exodus 4:13 NRSV). All excuses fail, so Moses is forced to come boldly to this statement. Many people dance around the truth and refuse to face up to their inner disobedience. It is vital that people realise the consequences of their refusal: if people will not go for God, then God cannot go. The gospel is carried by weak fallible human beings. This is within God's plan. God has to persuade and equip human beings to carry His presence and His word to the places that He has planned. If we do, it will be a blessing both to us and to those to whom we go. The gospel was taken to many parts of Asia and Africa only in the middle of the nineteenth century. One may ask why God waited so long, but it was God's people who waited.

God's answer is to reluctantly allow Moses to have Aaron his brother as a partner in ministry. Aaron would be the spokesman and be able to compensate for Moses' lack of confidence. As soon as Moses gained the confidence that God was with him, Aaron's role fades into the background.

God objected to Moses!

One of the most perplexing events in the life of Moses is that God intended to kill Moses for not circumcising his son. (Exodus 4:24-26). Circumcision was the covenant symbol of cutting off the power of the flesh and trusting in God alone. During the long conversation between Moses and God at the burning bush Moses did not confess this sin. This was the only true objection to his call, but Moses had either buried it deep in his heart, or had become hardened to his spiritual failure. But God could not allow him to go to His people with this radical disobedience. We often speak of the free will of man and forget the free will of God. We may choose, but the final choice always belongs with God.

Zipporah may have been part of the reason for his disobedience since she may have had a personal revulsion at the thought of circumcision. She circumcised the boy and threw the foreskin at the feet of her husband with a mocking rebuke

> *"Surely you are a husband of blood to me!" So He (God) let him go. Then she said, "You are a husband of blood!"-- because of the circumcision." (Exodus 4:25-26)*

So the issue was resolved and Zipporah brought Moses into line with the Abrahamic covenant of circumcision.

The ministry of Moses begins.

Moses went down to Egypt with a great message: *"Let my people go!"* (Exodus 5:1). He went down in the fullness of power and authority of God. Moses demonstrated miraculous power of an extraordinary nature. Few men are called to such a powerful ministry, and it is rare in the history of the Christian Church to see such revival power. God had made Moses to be nothing by long years of the discipline of loneliness in the wilderness with God. Now God made Moses into His friend and closest servant. Moses drew near to God and discovered the amazing truth that God was real and needed no human props to make His word and plan come into reality. God was demonstrating the full fruit of trusting in God alone.

Conclusion:

Moses demonstrates the amazing results when a person is brought to walk with God in intimate friendship. The path to attain this is marked with renunciation of rights and privileges, lonely vigils, suffering and deep breakings. God raised up Moses so that all his servants might learn these truths and become true servants of the king. Moses knew God intimately, but only in measure, and the glory of the New Testament is far surpassing that of the Old Covenant. While we learn from Moses, the disciple of Jesus Christ can enter in to an even deeper fellowship with God. How Moses would envy our generation and all the possibilities that are open to us through the death and resurrection of Jesus. At the same time he would have been surprised at the reluctance of many to forsake this present world's pleasures. The call of God demands all, and the early disciples forsook all to follow Christ and so showed us the way to know the power of being called as followers of the lamb.

CHAPTER 3

PAUL'S TEACHING ON LEADERSHIP

The writings of the apostle Paul contain essential wisdom on the subject of leadership. Paul gets to the very heart of this subject on many key issues.

1. A Leader's servant nature

Church history demonstrates that it is easy for leaderships to become elitist. On occasions leaders have kept themselves apart from the ordinary believers and encouraged the concept of a special group, living on a higher plane (clergy v laity). This has also on occasions led to models of leadership where the leader is given special privileges with a wealthy life-style. (Some bishops in the middle ages enjoyed lavish life styles while in recent years some preachers have flaunted an affluent life style as evidence of God's blessing and favour on their ministry). It is true that leaders should go ahead of the flock in their spiritual life and walk with God. But Paul teaches principles of servant leadership based not on elitism but on humility and compassionate care of the flock. The words he uses to describe leaders are very instructive:

- **Doulos – Slave**

  Doulos is the Greek word for a slave and is used by Paul to describe himself frequently (Titus 1:1; Galatians 1:10; Romans

1:1). Paul uses it to describe every servant of God (2 Timothy 2:24) and most importantly he says that Jesus Christ took on Himself the form of a slave (Philippians 2:7).

There are many implications:

- The word "slave" was not unknown in the time of Paul. There were 60 million slaves in the Roman empire making up a third of the total population of 180 million. Slaves were treated as possessions.

- A slave was owned by someone else! This means that Christ was owned by His Father, and Paul was owned by God. This is one of the key applications of the cross in our personal life. We are bought with a price and we no longer 'own' ourselves.

- A slave had no possessions of his own; he could not choose when he worked, when he had time off, what he wore, or where he lived. His whole life was an extension of his master's life.

- A slave had no wages, no rights.

- A slave was not responsible for his own upkeep. He was given all he needed for food, clothing and shelter. It was a secure life, but miserable unless his master was a just and caring person.

Paul describes himself as a bond slave of Jesus and he evidently enjoyed this position. Every leader must have the attitude of a loving slave to Jesus. Note that it is Christ, not the Church, who is our master. Leaders must serve humbly in the Church, as slaves who seek primarily to please their Master Jesus Christ, as they serve the people. A slave might serve food to guests, or wash the chariots of visitors, but his aim is not to impress them, but to please his master, who has given him the job to do and is watching how he does it. The slave may not even like some of the people he has to serve, but he does it well and gladly because he knows that his service will bring his master glory.

Illustration from the life of Helen Rosaveare

"On 15th January 1951 I returned to WEC Headquarters as a (missionary) candidate! On Tuesday after breakfast and washing up, I was told to go and wash the cement floor of the toilets and bathroom on the women candidates' floor. I found a bucket and a brush and set to. Strange as it may sound, it was almost the first time in my life that I had done a household chore. I was always the trainee-doctor till that moment! I scrubbed out the first toilet and started on the second. A candidate entered the first with muddy shoes. The floor was still wet. When she left, I returned and did the first again. Meanwhile, someone else entered the second. This continued some little time with a rising sense of frustration. I'd never get them clean! I'd fail, my very first day in training, to achieve the task I was set. Tears pricked at my eyes. I scrubbed on muttering, "Devil get out of here! Devil get out of here!"

There was a quiet spectator, Elizabeth who was in charge and had given me the task. She gently asked me why I was so upset. I explained the cause of my frustration.

"For whom are you scrubbing this floor?" she replied.

"Why for you of course; you sent me here." I've never forgotten her answer:

"No my dear, if you are doing it for me you may as well go home. You'll never satisfy me. You're doing it for the Lord and He saw the first time you cleaned it. That now is tomorrow's dirt.""

"Give me this mountain," Helen Rosaveare, p. 63.

When Christ washed the disciples' feet in the upper room in John 13, he dressed Himself as a slave and did the job of the lowest slave. Other slaves would prepare the bowl and the towels, but it was the lowest slave who would wash the guests' feet. Christ said that this was the pattern for His kingdom and that His disciples must do as He did. Evidently Paul viewed his ministry in a very humble light. The underlying truth of all this is that a leader is dispensable, and able to take orders without fearing for his reputation. He is a slave of Christ and most delighted to do His will.

- **Diakonos – servant**

This is the simple Greek word for a servant; it indicates something like a waiter, and refers quite frequently to those who serve at tables. It may come from an old Greek word "diako" meaning "to run errands". It is often thought that the seven men chosen in Acts 6 to serve at tables are the original pattern for the office of a deacon. Christ called Himself a 'deacon' in Matthew 20:26 and commanded His apostles to be servants to all. A waiter in a restaurant is the best picture. He is someone who attends to the needs of those who sit at table, watching for the moment that they will need him to serve them. Yet he does not intrude upon those he serves, but is self-effacing.

Women deacons.

When Paul describes the characteristics of a deacon in 1 Timothy 3:8-13 he includes a section on women (the Greek word "gune" may also be translated as wife). However on rare occasions there is controversy whether women may be deacons. In one way this is a question of translation. The English word "deacon" is a word borrowed from the Greek. But for the Greek reader it simply means "servant." To say that a woman may not be a deacon would be to maintain that she cannot be a servant in the Church!

Many assemblies would collapse if the women ceased to serve. Some may object that it is the office and title of "deacon" that women may not hold. Such an objection is to miss the whole point. Titles and office in the Church are secondary to the life that is laid down in service. It is a fact that Jesus was never ordained to any office or given an official title by any man. Among pioneers who changed the world such as Mary Slessor, Amy Carmichael and Gladys Aylward, the issue of the title they held was completely irrelevant to their life and work.

In Romans chapter 16 Paul greets 27 people by name, 10 of whom are women. But first he commends Phoebe to them, whom He describes as a "diakonos" a deacon of the Church in Cenchrea (Romans 16:1 - "diakonos" is in the masculine form, there is no feminine). He mentions Tryphena and Tryphosa who laboured much in the Lord (Romans 16:12). Paul evidently had no problem working with women, as he mentions in Philippians:

> *"And I urge you also, true companion, help these women who labored with me in the gospel, with Clement also, and the rest of my fellow workers, whose names are in the Book of Life." (Philippians 4:3)*

The word deacon refers most of all to the work of the ministry. As such some 95% of the work of leaders is serving and ministering. Some leaders meetings exclude deacons for no obvious reason since much of the work is done by deacons.

- **Uperetes – under-rower** (1 Corinthians 4:1).

This is the Greek word for an 'under-rower', who were the lowest workers on Roman ships. They were often despised criminals who were chained to their posts. There are two aspects of their service that have implications for God's servants. Firstly, they had no choice where they sat on the ship, and could not move around at their own will. God's servants must embrace the circumstances and co-workers that He has given us. Secondly, their attention had to be given to the task in hand, or the whole movement of the ship was affected. If they were distracted then the whole rhythm of the rowers could be broken as the oars struck each other. A drummer would maintain a steady beat, but one rower who lost pace with the others could bring the whole ship to a standstill or make it veer off course. Finally in a battle if the ship went down they were dead men, as they were chained to their posts. They died for those whom they served.

- ## Oikonomos – Steward

(1 Corinthians 4:1-2). This is the word for a steward of a large house. The householder would entrust the running of his house and the handling of his goods to this man. This means that God's servants have the keys to God's treasure house and food stores. We must be good stewards of the mysteries of God (1 Corinthians 4:1) and must feed the flock the right food at the right time.

> *"Who then is that faithful and wise steward, whom his master will make ruler over his household, to give them their portion of food in due season?" (Luke 12:42)*

- ## Episkopos – Overseer

  - **Watching for danger** - the word *episkopos* means an overseer, one who keeps watch. Elders are shepherds who must watch over their flocks. They are to be like the watchmen on the walls of Jerusalem, looking at the horizon for approaching danger.

- **Watching for God** - the elders on the watchtower, like Habakkuk, are there to hear what God will say to the flock, and to see what God wants to do among His people (Habakkuk 2:1).

- **Watching over people's souls**

"Obey those who have the rule over you, and be submissive, for they watch out for your souls, as those who must give account. Let them do so with joy and not with grief, for that would be unprofitable for you." *(Hebrews 13:17)*

Elders must be vigilant about the things that are happening in the lives of their flock. They must be aware of wrong doctrines coming in, and of people's carnal ambitions. They must watch to try and correct these things before they take a hold.

▪ **Presbuteros** - Elder.

This is one of the most common words for a leader and it occurs at least 61 times in the New Testament. (The second word for elder, 'episkopos' - overseer, occurs a mere 5 times.) It occurs at least 61 times in English translation, but it is found in other places in the Greek such as "Your old men ("presbuterous" – elders) shall dream dreams" in Acts 2:17). It means literally 'an older man' but the force of the word does not lie merely in being older. This can never in itself be a foundation for office in the Church. The word indicates all the positive virtues associated with age - maturity, experience and wisdom, to name but a few.

The opposite would be the term 'young man'. The qualities of youth that cannot bear office are impetuosity, inexperience, immaturity etc. Churches cannot be led by inexperienced or immature people but they can be led by mature young men such as Timothy (1 Timothy 4:12). The Holy Spirit takes up the wisdom of experience, and produces men of stature, able to lead and guide the Church. The role of elders then, is to offer the covering of spiritual wisdom and maturity. The expectation of God is that all believers will move steadily into the maturity of being fathers and mothers in Christ, and will begin to share in some measure in the leadership of the local assembly, taking responsibility seriously, and in a sober manner. The body of elders in a growing congregation should be increasing.

The key thing at this point is to distinguish between the call and anointing to lead which makes a man a leader among elders, and the quality of spiritual maturity that makes a man an elder.

The distinction between leadership and eldership is very important. They overlap, but it is important that younger believers with leadership potential realise they can operate in spiritual gifts and ministries long before they are recognised and appointed to some office. The strict division of clergy and laity is a dangerous one and by it some may lose their confidence to minister.

This distinction is also important because not all elders are leaders. Leadership is rare and to be nourished and encouraged wherever it is found. It would be wrong for elders to merely manage the Church. Management is not in itself leadership, and it is much more common to find managers in positions of authority rather than visionary leaders.

2. The work of a Leader.

Paul uses four main concepts to describe the work of a leader.

- **Stratiotes – Soldier**

   Paul is the only writer of the New Testament to use the image of a soldier to describe ministers and Christians. He calls Epaphroditus and Archippus his "fellow soldiers" (Philippians 2:25; Philemon verse 2).
   He challenges Timothy:

   > *"You therefore must endure hardship as a good soldier of Jesus Christ. No one engaged in warfare entangles himself with the affairs of this life, that he may please him who enlisted him as a soldier."*
   > *(2 Timothy 2:3-4)*

   The servant of God is a soldier. The Christian soldier does not fight with carnal weapons:

   > *"For though we walk in the flesh, we do not war according to the flesh. For the weapons of our warfare are not carnal but mighty in God for pulling down strongholds, casting down arguments and every high thing that exalts itself against the knowledge of God, bringing every thought into captivity to the obedience of Christ."*
   > *(2 Corinthians 10:3-5)*

   Christians are in a battle against the powers of darkness not against human beings:

   > *"For we do not wrestle against flesh and blood, but against principalities, against powers, against the rulers of the darkness of this age, against spiritual hosts of wickedness in the heavenly places."*
   > *(Ephesians 6:12)*

The Christian is conscious of this battle and that there are unseen forces of evil behind the visible world. Christians will experience resistance in their prayer life and discouraging thoughts. They are to fight in this realm to maintain a positive attitude.

If a leader forgets he or she is in a warfare, then the battle is lost at that point. Christians must not just shout slogans about their victory, they must knuckle down and fight. Yes the war has been won, but there will be many "mopping up" battles before that victorious position has been fully realized. The sad truth is that Satan can get a victory, but only when God's servants give up the fight. Giving up the fight may be for many reasons. Some grow tired and discouraged and just withdraw from prayer and witnessing. Others become superficial and worldly and simply begin to enjoy the passing pleasures of this world. The axiom *"Evil triumphs when good men do nothing"* is never truer than in respect to the dimension of Christian warfare. Churches that have grown cold or casual in their prayer lives will often be able to trace this back to indifference in the leadership. Some Christians simply do not engage in warfare. Some polish their doctrines endlessly, always seeking to prove others are wrong or have some nuance of error. While sound doctrine is to be cherished, this must not be at the expense of giving up on the fight.

In reading the prophet Jeremiah one becomes conscious that the priests and elders of Israel had ceased to fight. In one terrible cry straight from the heart of God, Jeremiah declares:

> *"For death has come through our windows, has entered our palaces, to kill off the children-- no longer to be outside! And the young men-- no longer on the streets!" (Jeremiah 9:21)*

The force of this wail is that the enemy has entered into the very homes of God's people. In this day 'wolves and lions' have entered into Churches and homes and destroyed the moral and spiritual life of many. One of the chief functions of a leader is to lead into battle against the enemy of our souls.

■ **Poimen – Shepherd.**

This word is translated pastor in Ephesians 4:11. It appears as a verb in Acts 20:28-29:

> *"Therefore take heed to yourselves and to all the flock, among which the Holy Spirit has made you overseers, to shepherd/pastor the Church of God which He purchased with His own blood. For I know this, that after my departure savage wolves will come in among you, not sparing the flock."*

There is an immediate connection between this and the soldier concept of leadership. The shepherd must fight the wolves that would destroy the flock. Jesus said:

> *"I am the good shepherd. The good shepherd gives His life for the sheep. But a hireling, he who is not the shepherd, one who does not own the sheep, sees the wolf coming and leaves the sheep and flees; and the wolf catches the sheep and scatters them. The hireling flees because he is a hireling and does not care about the sheep."*
> *(John 10:11-13)*

The shepherd fights because of love and his greatest weapon is that he is willing to die for the sheep. This is the most challenging dimension of a leader's work. Not all leaders have the ministry of a pastor/shepherd, but all leaders are to have a shepherd's heart.

David had the heart of a true shepherd and as a young man he fought the bears and the lions that would attack the flock. From this we understand that David did not fight Goliath for prestige but for love of the flock that would be scattered and destroyed if the Philistines prevailed. Attacking a lion or a bear was an act of indescribable courage and this is the heart of God as revealed in Christ. Amos was a shepherd and describes the act of saving an impossibly wounded lamb from the mouth of a lion:

> *"As a shepherd takes from the mouth of a lion two legs or a piece of an ear..." (Amos 3:12)*

Such an act is a waste of the shepherd's life unless there is hope of restoring the lamb to life. Christ died for ruined sinners with no human hope of healing. When a person is in a coma the last sensory perception is the ear, and the last means of communication is to flutter the eyelids or to squeeze the hand. When a human life is damaged beyond hope, as long as there is an ability to hear the word of Jesus, and to respond in the heart, then He is able to restore that life to a perfect state. Every pastor/shepherd in the Church must seek to receive from Jesus the courage to risk his life for the flock, and the hope that however bad a state he comes across, Jesus is able to heal and restore to the image of God.

The shepherd heart is the foundation of all ongoing ministry. Human souls are as timid as birds and will fly away and shut their door if frightened. It is the Christ like quality of gentleness that convinces people it is safe to open up and entrust their inner secrets.

Ultimately there is no one quite like Jesus Christ. There are some choice men and women who have touched deep wells of His love, but there is no one else who can handle our inner lives like He does. It is for this reason that shepherds must grasp that their ministry does not lie in getting people to open up to them, but rather to Him.

- ### Georgos – Farmer

The metaphor of farming is at the heart of the ministry and of many of the parables and teachings of Jesus. When Jesus said that His father is the vine dresser (John 15:1) He used this word "georgos" which is from the root word "geo" meaning soil or earth (c.f. the English "geography" and "geology"). God then is a farmer and He keeps sheep and tends vines. Jesus is the vine and we are the branches (John 15:5).

The first point of this metaphor is that farming is a work of patience. The farmer chooses good seed and then maintains the best conditions for it to flourish, and so it is with leaders in God's vineyard. Their work is to keep sowing the word of the kingdom (Matthew 13:19) and to keep exhorting the hearers to keep their hearts in the right attitude for the word to grow and bear fruit. As Jesus said in John 15:4 the branches cannot bear fruit of themselves. They must abide in Christ, in His presence.

The second lesson of this metaphor is that leaders cannot produce growth or fruit or any crop without the help of God. The vine is the most common metaphor for the kingdom of God. A vine is a weak tree, unlike the mighty cedar of Lebanon or the great oaks of England. The vine needs a trellis to support the branches, and the true Vine – Jesus Christ hung on the cross to produce the fruit of eternal life. So too the Christian leader must be crucified with Christ and find the place of entire dependence on Jesus. He must depend on His word, His presence, His love and His strength. Of all lessons this is the hardest: that God does not require our intelligence, our natural gifts and abilities, He requires our weakness. Whether we have many gifts or few, when we are weak and depend on Jesus then God takes up our lives and suffuses them with His own life and so brings glory to Himself.

Finally Paul uses the metaphor of farming to encourage the leaders to go on with Christ themselves.

"The hard-working farmer must be first to partake of the crops."
(2 Timothy 2:6)

By this Paul is referring to the fact that leaders don't only tell others what to do, they also do it themselves! It is a simple but common error among leaders to give the impression that they are above the flock, superior in spirituality, holiness, prayerfulness and devotion. Such leaders will frequently tell their flocks what to do, but the godly leader will include himself in this challenge and respond himself to the challenges he presents to the flock.

- ## Athleo – Athlete

"Do you not know that those who run in a race all run, but one receives the prize? Run in such a way that you may obtain it. And everyone who competes for the prize is temperate in all things. Now they do it to obtain a perishable crown, but we for an imperishable crown. Therefore I run thus: not with uncertainty. Thus I fight: not as one who beats the air. But I discipline my body and bring it into subjection, lest, when I have preached to others, I myself should become disqualified." (1 Corinthians 9:24-27)
"And also if anyone competes in athletics, he is not crowned unless he competes according to the rules." (2 Timothy 2:4-6)

The chief image here is that of the marathon runner (see also Hebrews 12:1). But Paul also uses the image of the boxer – not beating the air but landing a few well aimed punches; and then the wrestler (Ephesians 6:12). Athletes must be disciplined in the way they treat their body, not overeating, keeping fit and trim. Spiritually, believers must keep their excess weight down and not be burdened with the cares and lusts of the world. To be spiritually agile our hearts must be free of the clutter of worldly desires and cares.

> *England footballer Sir Stanley Matthews died on 23 February 2000. He was 85 years old and had jogged every morning and never eaten anything that would cause him to put on weight. He fasted once a week. He was a true athlete. His wife said that he kept thinking he was only 55 years old.*

3. Paul's teaching on the Leader and Money

Paul believed that pastors were to be supported by the offerings of the local Church. In 1 Corinthians 9 he explains that soldiers, farm workers and shepherds must get some profit from their work, even if it is just the milk from the flock (v. 7). He quotes the Old Testament that even the ox treading out the corn must eat, and is allowed to eat the corn it is walking on (v. 9).

There is little controversy in the concept of pastors and leaders being supported by the Church, and there will be different methods for that support according to how the Lord leads different ministries. However, the interesting thing is that Paul himself declined to accept financial support. 1 Corinthians 9 is Paul's account of his determination to remain free from the snares that can result from receiving pay from the Church. In a way, the snares are obvious, but they still need to be stated:

- **Paul was determined to make sure that the gospel was preached without charge.** He did not want anyone to think that the gospel would be preached for financial reward.

   "What is my reward then? That when I preach the gospel, I may present the gospel of Christ without charge, that I may not abuse my authority in the gospel." (1 Corinthians 9:18)

On October 28th. 1741 George Whitefield, left Edinburgh in the company of a friend, riding a horse given to him by Lord Leven. As he and his friend rode through the wild border country they came to a village where they met a widow woman whose goods were about to be confiscated for debt, so George gave her five gold guineas. His friend remonstrated, saying it was more than he could properly afford. He got the reply, with the affectionate smile which erased any impression of smugness: "When God brings a case of distress before us, it is that we may relieve it."

They rode on into the hills. A highwayman sprang out at them, pistol cocked. They had no escape. The highwayman cantered off with the contents of their pockets. George could not resist a dig at his friend: "Was it not better the widow had those five guineas than the thief?"

Suddenly they heard the gallop of hooves behind them. They reined in and to their dismay saw the highwayman again, who shouted at George: "Give me your coat, it is better than mine."

They rode on once more with George wearing a tattered garment smelling of whiskey. About ten minutes later they heard hooves again, coming yet more furiously. This time they could see some cottages down below them, not far off, and fearing lest the highwayman meant to kill them for their horses (Lord Leven's gift was a fine sleek animal) the two fled for their lives, pursued with blood curdling yells, "Stop! Stop!"

They reached the cottages where the highwayman dared not follow.

When Whitefield took off the filthy coat he found why the man had yelled for them to stop.

A purse containing a hundred guineas was sewn into the lining.

(George Whitefield and the Great Awakening,
by John Pollock pp 185-6.)

Jesus said *"Freely you have received, freely give" (Matthew 10:8)* and the word "freely" does not mean liberally, it means "as a free gift" (Greek "dorean").

- **Ministers must not be greedy for gain.** Paul describes in Acts 20:33-35 that he worked to support others and himself. He had demonstrated generosity, and a willingness to work hard with his hands. When Paul quotes Jesus *"It is more blessed to give than to receive," (Acts 20:35)* he is addressing the elders of the large Church at Ephesus.

  "Yes, you yourselves know that these hands have provided for my necessities, and for those who were with me. I have shown you in every way, by labouring like this, that you must support the weak. And remember the words of the Lord Jesus, that He said, "It is more blessed to give than to receive."" (Acts 20:34-35)

  Paul felt it was necessary that ministers be enabled to be givers and not just receivers of money.

- **Ministers must be careful not to become servants of people.** In Galatians 1:10 Paul states that if he were a people-pleaser he would cease to be the servant of Christ. Salaries can have this effect, and in some sad cases, Churches have withheld the salary of the pastor if they were unhappy with his preaching. Pastors and leaders must be accountable but they must also know that they are not preaching to please people, but God who called them.

- **The love of money can destroy a ministry.** In 1 Timothy 6:6-10 Paul describes the danger of loving money. When blessing comes through a leader's ministry, people will offer him gifts - sometimes very large gifts. Paul says that the love of money is a root of all kinds of evil, but mainly that it produces all kinds of lusts, which in turn cause people to be pierced with sorrows.

- **The sin of Balaam.** Balaam was invited to assist Balak in cursing Israel, but God commanded him not to go (Numbers 22:12). Then Balak renewed the invitation by sending important princes, to impress Balaam with a promise of great financial reward (Numbers 22:15-17). God told Balaam to go with them if they invited him again in the morning. But Balaam was so filled with lust for the reward that he did not wait for the princes to invite him, but simply went with them. God was merciful to Balaam and did not slay him, and spoke faithfully through him. But Balaam sold his soul to sinful men to co-operate with them for financial gain.

- **The doctrine of Balaam** (Numbers 31:16). The result was that, in the end, Balaam was completely corrupted; he advised Balak that the only way to defeat Israel was to entice the people to commit sin, by bowing down to the Midianite idols and committing fornication with the Midianite women (Numbers 25:1-2). The result was that Israel lost its spiritual authority, until Phinehas put an end to the corruption by his act of executing a guilty couple. Jesus warned the Church at Pergamos that they were allowing this kind of ministry to continue in that Church. It would be characterized by:

  • Indicating to believers that it is not a sin to sleep together before marriage, and that the occasional sexual transgression is normal.

  • A seeking to 'smooth out' the difficulties for people to be Church members, by diluting the New Testament standards of righteousness and holiness.

- Omitting to preach strongly against sin in the Church; perhaps focusing on subjects such as the Second Coming or prosperity, but neglecting personal holiness.

In his book, "The Happiest People on Earth" Demos Shakarian recalls how a certain evangelist came to preach at one of his crusades. Although his preaching was good, Demos became uneasy about his avid interest in the offerings. Demos had agreed with him on payments for his preaching role but on the last night the evangelist extended the offering time repeatedly by calling people forward to give again and again. When he'd squeezed every last dollar from their pockets, he collected all the cash and stuffed it all in the bag he'd brought to the crusade for this purpose. Demos was aghast but he felt not to stop the man. God spoke to his heart, "do not touch my anointed". Six years later he met the man. He had lost his ministry and also lost all his money. He came to Demos' office to ask for the fare to get to Detroit. He was reduced to poverty. Three years later Demos heard that he had died.

God honours His word spoken by fallible human vessels, but there is a heavy personal price to pay for leaving the way of righteousness.

- **The sin of Judas.**

Paul expected the highest standards from a leader of God in matters pertaining to money. The worst example in the whole Bible is that of Judas, who was called to be an apostle. Some have speculated that, when Judas fell, Paul was ultimately given his ministry. If this is the case then Judas might have had the most prominent ministry of all the apostles if he had not fallen.

Judas was simply a thief, and he saw that his position could make him rich (John 12:6). He stole from the bag of offerings that were given directly to Jesus by those He ministered to. Judas took from this money, and finally sold Jesus for 30 pieces of silver. Some have speculated that Judas thought that Jesus would exhibit further authority, and escape by some supernatural means. Whatever the case, he was blinded by the possibility of earning some money for nothing. He betrayed Jesus, but he also betrayed himself by selling his soul and his conscience in order to obtain money. All ministers must fear the thin end of the wedge. It is easy to exaggerate and even lie in order to impress congregations and obtain money.

4. The Leader and Other Ministries

Paul had respect for other ministries. He always travelled with other ministers like Barnabas and Silas. He gave honour to the different ministries of people such as Peter and Apollos (1 Corinthians 3:3). Leaders should promote other ministries, not just their own.

Of all the Christ like characteristics leaders are to embrace this may be the hardest and therefore also the rarest of qualities. Paul said:

> *"Let nothing be done through selfish ambition or conceit, but in lowliness of mind let each esteem others better than himself. Let each of you look out not only for his own interests, but also for the interests of others." (Philippians 2:3-4)*

He commends Timothy who had this attitude:

"But I trust in the Lord Jesus to send Timothy to you shortly, that I also may be encouraged when I know your state. For I have no one like-minded, who will sincerely care for your state. For all seek their own, not the things which are of Christ Jesus." (Philippians 2:19-21).

Ministers are not to be competitive for that would be to wreak havoc and destruction in the body of Christ.

5. The Leader and Suffering

"Life is not as idle ore,
But iron dug from central gloom,
And heated hot with burning fears,
And dipt in baths of hissing tears,
And batter'd with the shocks of doom,
To shape and use." Alfred Lord Tennyson

Some have interpreted the gospel to mean that if we have faith we will enjoy health, prosperity and be free of the accidents and difficulties that beset the rest of mankind. But Paul suffered terrible beatings, stoning, shipwrecks and other traumas for the sake of the gospel (2 Corinthians 11:23-33 and 12:1-10). He saw a clear relationship between spiritual power and suffering. He believed that through weakness God would keep him in the attitude and position in which he could be used. This principle of ministry is brought out in 2 Corinthians:

➤ *"Yes, we had the sentence of death in ourselves, that we should not trust in ourselves but in God who raises the dead." 2 Corinthians 1:9.*

➤ *"...always carrying about in the body the dying of the Lord Jesus, that the life of Jesus also may be manifested in our body." 2 Corinthians 4:10 see also verses 7-12 of the same chapter.*

> ➤ *"And lest I should be exalted above measure by the abundance of the revelations, a thorn in the flesh was given to me, a messenger of Satan to buffet me, lest I be exalted above measure. Concerning this thing I pleaded with the Lord three times that it might depart from me. And He said to me, "My grace is sufficient for you, for My strength is made perfect in weakness." Therefore most gladly I will rather boast in my infirmities, that the power of Christ may rest upon me. Therefore I take pleasure in infirmities, in reproaches, in needs, in persecutions, in distresses, for Christ's sake. For when I am weak, then I am strong. 2 Corinthians 12:7-10.*

Paul saw suffering as an essential aspect of the ministry. The deeper and greater the ministry, the more the suffering! In this light, it should provoke a deep humility in God's servants, and a realisation that some who suffer persecution may know the Lord in greater depth than many others who have all the comforts of modern life. Equally it is of vital importance to realise that suffering in all its forms is allowed of God to release the perfume of Christ from the depths of our hearts. Paul declares in 2 Corinthians that our frail humanity is like an alabaster box containing priceless perfume. Paul said that "we have this treasure in earthen vessels." As the vessel is broken so the perfume is released.

The story on the following two pages is from our first years as a missionary couple in Cameroon, West Africa:

****

It was December 1980. The little Church in Nkongsamba, Cameroon was just over a year old. Among the group of believers was a young man named Felix, an outstanding student at the Lycee. We took him with others to a Christian convention in the south west province about a hundred kilometres away. The Saturday afternoon of the convention Vicki and I were praying in our room in the sweltering tropical heat, getting ready to preach when suddenly we heard shouting "Come quick, the boys are dying!" We ran out to find the vice principal of the Mission looking shaken. "Quick! Down by the river!" he shouted. We got in the car with him and a few others and drove the mile down to a house which was right by a fast flowing river. Felix was staying here with other young men. They had been playing with a ball in the river - little knowing how deep and fast flowing it was, due to a small hydro-electric turbine 300m upstream. The swirling water had cut a channel in the middle of the river 6m deep. One person had got into trouble and had been sucked under, then a second had gone in to help, followed by a third and a fourth. All had been sucked under. Vicki recognised Felix's clothes in a pile by the river. Grief stricken we dragged one of the young men from the river. I gave him mouth to mouth resuscitation. We struggled on and on, one missionary got an oxygen tank from his workshop. For a while we could feel a faint pulse, but we failed to revive him. We learned that Felix had already been dragged out and someone had sped off to the hospital with him 40km away, but without attempting resuscitation. After some time we headed for the hospital. His body was in the mortuary, and at that time there was no cooling system. The mortuary was set well apart.

We sent a message to Felix's father. He had been involved in gun running for an insurgency and had been imprisoned for five years back in the 1970's. He arrived with ten men at 3am seeking answers and vengeance. As he approached the house we were staying in God spoke to him not to harm us. The men stood around waiting for his word to attack us, but it never came. It was the first of many miracles.

We took him to see Felix: the body was already badly decomposed. There were tears and wails of grief. It took a further 12 hours to get the body ready and a coffin made. We drove back to Nkongsamba carrying the body in our VW bus. The family were gathering. When we arrived at the home of Felix there was a crowd of hundreds of angry men who had heard of the accident. They held stones and machetes. A stone flew and smashed the wing mirror of the VW bus. It was a tense moment as the mother of Felix wailed and lamented in front of us. More stones flew. Again Felix's father intervened and begged the crowd to leave us alone. He decided his son should be buried in his village some 75km away, and we set off again.

After the burial, some of the young converts were beaten and forbidden to attend the little Church. The false rumour had been spread that we had drowned them in baptism. Many enquirers simply melted away. The Church was an object of anger and derision. Once during a prayer meeting someone threw a fire-ball into the meeting. We were all unharmed on that occasion.

In this atmosphere of oppressive opposition the faithful little band of believers gathered. We could not evangelise, we could not simply carry on as if nothing had happened. So we prayed. We were some 15 believers pressed into a path of prayer. We held a week of prayer and fasting, meeting daily at 7am for an hour then 12 noon and then 7pm. Then a few weeks later we held another and so on for a year. Without knowing what was happening God dug deep in our hearts and lives and released a depth of peace and anointing that we could never have dreamed possible. We had been led to death, and then discovered that it was a doorway to life.

It was a year perhaps before the Church began to grow again. But then the Spirit of the Lord was upon us in a fragrance and power that melted us. God had laid foundations that went deep. Felix's father became a friend. He read a journal that his son had written and wept as he realised the deep transformation that had taken place in his son's heart before he died. Ten years later Felix's father gave himself to the Lord and joined our little Church, perhaps a crowning miracle among so many. He died some 10 years ago now and has joined his son in heaven.   *Les and Vicki Wheeldon*

****

As God's people seek to become ministers of Christ it is vital that we do not seek the path of ease and comfort as the will of God. Paul said:

> *"Nor do I count my life dear to myself, so that I may finish my race with joy, and the ministry which I received from the Lord Jesus, to testify to the gospel of the grace of God." (Acts 20:24)*

Conclusion

It is so easy for Churches and ministers to unconsciously imbibe the spirit of the world and allow it to shape our model of Christian ministry and the Church. How different is the kingdom of God. When Christ heard His disciples arguing about who was to be the greatest in the kingdom of God he called a little child and set him in the midst. and said,

> *"Assuredly, I say to you, unless you are converted and become as little children, you will by no means enter the kingdom of heaven. Therefore whoever humbles himself as this little child is the greatest in the kingdom of heaven." (Matthew 18:3-4).*

The goal of every leader is to bring the fragrance of a kingdom where different values operate, where humility, selfless love and grace are the most prized qualities. May God raise up many leaders who by word and action display the wonders of that kingdom.

PART II

~

APOSTLES AND SPIRITUAL LEADERSHIP

"Until self-effacing men return again to spiritual leadership, we may expect a progressive deterioration in the quality of popular Christianity, year after year till we reach the point where the grieved Holy Spirit withdraws — like the Shekinah from the temple."
A.W. Tozer

CHAPTER 4

APOSTLES: A PATTERN FOR LEADERSHIP

An apostle is a leader chosen of God to bring the key revelation of Christ to the Church. As such their ministry is foundational, both in the formation of Churches and the ongoing development of them. The word "leader" is not frequently used in the Bible, but there is no doubt that apostles were leaders in the New Testament Church. The term "apostle" indicates a dimension of inspiring ministry and leadership that shows the Church the way forward. Many men have had such a clear calling and gifting including Wesley, Luther, Finney etc. Many missionary pioneers have perhaps been apostles including Hudson Taylor, C.T. Studd and many others. The Greek word means "one sent" which is the literal meaning of the word "missionary" though it would be wrong to equate every missionary as being "apostolic."

In studying the apostles as a pattern for leadership it will be objected to by many that there are very few apostles in the body of Christ. There were certainly more than 12 apostles in the first century. Paul and Barnabas were apostles (Acts 14:14). Epaphroditus and Titus are also called apostles in Philippians 2:25 and 2 Corinthians 8:23 (translated messenger.) There is moreover no biblical reason to believe that the office of apostle ended in the first century. It is true that the New Testament canon was completed in the first century, but it was not written exclusively by apostles. Luke, Mark and James (the brother of Jesus not the brother of John) were not apostles. This word has become synonymous with being a "spiritual giant" which does not help us grasp the true meaning of this ministry. There have been, and always will be, great evangelists, Bible teachers and apostles, but there are thousands of evangelists, teachers and apostles whose ministry is not so prominent.

But are there apostles today and is it important to recognize them? There are surely many apostles in the Churches today, but recognizing them does not seem to be of vital importance and would probably be controversial and unprofitable in the long run given the heavy connotations associated with the word in the English language. Though the use of the title may be unhelpful, it is nevertheless vital to discern and receive the kind of ministry that has an apostolic dimension. Jesus commended the Church in Ephesus:

> *"And you have tested those who say they are apostles and are not, and have found them liars." (Revelation 2:2)*

This verse indicates that the Church in Ephesus knew what an apostle was. This is vital if we are to identify those who are false apostles (2 Corinthians 11:13).

Despite these reservations about the use of the word "apostle" it will be agreed that the way God prepared and used the apostles is a foundational lesson for the way God prepares and uses all His leaders. Apostolic ministry should be pursued by the whole Church. Though it may be rare for one man to contain such a depth and a fullness of ministry yet that depth and fullness is the goal of all ministers and Christians in some degree or other. It is as we understand apostolic gifting that we realize our need of this brand of ministry to touch the Church as a whole.

In studying the apostolic calling it is hoped that all who serve God will be stirred to grasp this high calling that undergirds the apostolic dimension of leadership.

What about women?

There is no mention of any female apostles in the New Testament (or of women elders for that matter). Jesus, who was no stranger to conflict, treated women with dignity and respect, but still chose twelve men to be His twelve apostles even though there were a number of women travelling with His group of disciples (Luke 8:1-3). Some have argued that Romans 16:7 is referring to a female apostle named Junia:

> *"Greet Andronicus and Junia, my countrymen and my fellow prisoners, who are of note among the apostles, who also were in Christ before me." (Romans 16:7)*

This verse has three possible meanings:
1. Junia was an apostle.
2. Andronicus and Junia were a married couple who were well known to the apostles.
3. Andronicus was an apostle and that he functioned as a team with his wife.

Whichever of these three interpretations is chosen, this verse on its own is a slim foundation for such an important doctrine.

So can a woman be an apostle or a leader in the Church? There are many examples from Church history (Catherine Booth, Mary Slessor, Amy Carmichael, Jackie Pullinger) but none in the New Testament. The Bible teaches that men are to shoulder responsibility and authority in the home and in the Church. But is this the final word?

The Leadership of Deborah

Deborah, although in the Old Testament, is a clear exception to this rule. What then are the implications of the Bible's description of the life and rule of Deborah in Israel in the time of the judges?

Firstly, Deborah contradicts the idea that women are easily deceived and/or emotionally unstable. Not only was Deborah calm and steadfast in the face of traumatic circumstances, but nearly all the male leaders in the book of Judges were unstable and deceived by pride and other sins. Samson was prey to sexual lust (Judges 16:1); Jephthah was impulsive and unwise in his vow to God (Judges 11:30-34); Gideon ended up worshipping the idols he had once destroyed (Judges 8:27). Later on in the history of God's people, all the kings of the northern kingdom of Israel were evil men, while Saul, David and Solomon and most of the kings of Judah had major flaws of character.

Secondly, Deborah honoured the men by urging Barak to lead the army of Israel into battle. Barak declined and Deborah warned him that the honour of slaying the enemy Sisera would go to a woman. Deborah's leadership was not based on reckless ambition but she was deferential and able to encourage others to take a part that would outshine her role. One might wish that many male leaders would follow her example.

Conclusion: It is easy to miss the wisdom of God in including Deborah in the annals of Israel's history. This whole episode teaches that though God has chosen men (with all their imperfections) to bear responsibility, yet there are exceptions to this rule and God is able to raise up godly, faithful women (who may also on occasions have imperfections!) to bear burdens in God's kingdom. It is vital for men not to have their minds closed to the possibility that women may fulfil a significant leading role in the work of the kingdom.

Paradoxically many men have no problem in recognising women in leadership so long as they leave their country and serve in some remote mission field. It may be argued that countless women have often laboured without much recognition in extremely hostile circumstances to bring the gospel to the lost.

There are also many circumstances in which women have been forced to take leadership roles. In communist states many pastors and leaders were imprisoned leaving the work to be carried on by godly women. In some western denominations so few men attend Churches that the women are in a majority and are compelled to stand in the gap.

The vital lesson from the life of Deborah is to refuse all gender stereotyping, and to be open to recognise God's hand in the life of a person whatever their gender.

The need for leadership qualities in all.

There is an old axiom that "there are too many chiefs and not enough Indians!" It might be readily agreed that in many Churches there are far too many critics and not enough followers. But there can never be enough godly leaders. A truly godly leader will never cause division or trouble for a trivial or a selfish reason, but will support and promote the unity of the body of Christ. Moreover, every person who has truly spiritual qualities of leadership will find that he or she is inspiring others to follow in their footsteps. (True leaders produce more leaders not just more followers!) Every individual in Christ's body needs to understand the keys to leadership since everyone will function to a greater or lesser degree in this vital area. A Sunday school teacher will inspire their class, a student will make decisions that will challenge and convict his peers. A mother will impact her children with her devotion to Christ and lead them to salvation and a deeper walk with God. A businessman will impress his colleagues with standards and behaviour that make him stand out a mile from others. This is not to mention those who will lead prayer meetings, evangelistic movements, Churches, conventions and seminars in a manner that will change lives forever in their generation. Not all are called to be apostles, but all can bear the stamp of our chief apostle Jesus Christ:

"Therefore holy brethren, partakers of the heavenly calling, consider the Apostle and High Priest of our confession, Christ Jesus." Hebrews 3:1.

Apostolic or Christian qualities?

There are many aspects to the lessons that Jesus taught His apostles that are actually for all believers. The apostles were most frequently referred to as disciples (Mark 8:23; Matthew 10:1). As Jesus taught the twelve the foundations of the kingdom, many of the lessons were simply truths that all believers must learn and assimilate. In this respect leaders of all kinds are to be examples to the Church of how to grow in Christ.

The vanity of titles.

It is a sad dimension of leadership in the modern Church that titles and academic honours are so ardently sought after.

"Someone commented that the fervent heat of the Welsh revival was lost by 'degrees!'"

The two most frequently used words for a Christian in the New Testament are "saint" meaning a "holy person" and "disciple" which means "student" or "learner." These refer not to the beliefs of the person but to the life-style of the individual. Similarly it would be sad to have the title of "pastor" and yet to be lacking in love. An adjective is invariably a better description of a person than a title. "He is very loving," "She is very caring," are words that describe a person with pastoral gifting. To bear the title means nothing without the appropriate qualities of character. It is amusing how titles quickly become meaningless. So a person may claim to be "Pentecostal" or "Apostolic" or "Methodist" while not thinking in the slightest of how they match up in their personal life to the qualities these words are referring to.

There are many different words used in the New Testament for leaders, including: apostles, prophets, evangelists, pastors, teachers, elders and deacons. In seeking to understand the different aspects of leadership in the New Testament it is important to distinguish between (a) elders and deacons and (b) the five-fold ministries through which the Church is to be built up. If one were to insist on an idealistic interpretation of scripture, the word "pastor" would be used to describe the ministry of an individual and not their leadership status in the Church. However, idealistic or legalistic attention to biblically correct leadership structures will nearly always miss the point. The Bible is not essentially concerned with titles and structures, but with character. It is more important to cultivate right attitudes than right structures. A man may be an elder in a leadership team, and dominate the others with harsh methods or a dominant character. He may manipulate the team around his own will through cleverness and shrewd politics. Another man may be a pastor with all the levers of control in his hands, but yet be genuinely submitted to a group of men with whom he works.

Eldership: Biblical leadership structure.

The Churches of the New Testament were led by elders. These men were chosen for their godly character, not their ministry (1 Timothy 3:1-7). Two apostles referred to themselves as elders as well as apostles (2 John verse 1; 1 Peter 5:1). Interestingly, Paul never refers to himself as an elder which may mean he never saw himself in that role. It would certainly be wrong to assume that all apostles are elders.

There are many different ministries that bless the body of Christ, but the authority in the assembly lies in a body of elders to whom all ministers are submitted. It may be assumed that those who have a gift of apostleship, healing, pastoring, evangelism, teaching etc... should normally be elders in the body of Christ. There are also exceptions where some ministers have shown great gift but have some manifest weakness of character. Such will find safety in functioning in their ministry, while being accountable to a body of elders.

The interface between eldership and gifting is a common cause of strain in Churches. This is because a very gifted man will often become very authoritative in the Church. It is the reason that most Churches function on a model of following one charismatic leader. It is also a fact of an eldership structure that it can paralyze the Church by restraining gifted men from taking a lead. Leadership by a committee will often result in a watering down of vision.

However changing structures will rarely deal with the spiritual lacks that are at the heart of most problems in Churches. It is for this reason that the vital role of apostles be recognized. Apostles are not chief administrators of local Churches, but are men of vision who inspire the believers to know Christ and serve Him. A Church may have perfect structures, but may be in terminal decline because it lacks apostolic vision. It is this vision and ministry that lifts the believers to fulfil their calling. Elderships do well to ensure that they either have apostolic ministry or are seeking to introduce it to the Churches over which they hold responsibility.

It is not profitable for men to seek the title of an apostle, as that would be the vainest quest in the world. Firstly, the title is of itself meaningless, it must be backed up by a ministry and spiritual understanding that are life-changing and inspirational. Secondly, apostles are made by God not man (Galatians 1:1). So why discuss apostleship? The answer is that while we may not aspire to the title, we may freely aspire to have some dimension of this ministry in our lives. Just as we thirst for the prophetic dimension in evangelism, teaching and healing, so we are to seek the apostolic dimension to the Church's ministry. We must see what apostolic leadership qualities are, so that we may actively seek that ministry that makes the body of Christ come alive.

What about the foot soldiers?

I am compelled at this point to interject a word of advice to those believers who are in troubled Churches either led by strong men who won't listen, or by a committee that has no vision. On rare occasions Churches are grieving the Holy Spirit in a way that makes attending meetings an ordeal. The answer is to pray. Leaders have access to the administrative levers of power, but everyone can by-pass the junior leaders and talk directly to the King. He may direct believers to patient praying and waiting for Him to act, or He may direct them to join another Church. But the key thing to remember is that all believers are to manifest another kingdom just as much as the leaders. Whatever the King may show us to do, it is certain that He will require humility, love and grace in all our words and actions.

Apostles/leaders – on display.

"For I think that God has displayed us, the apostles, last, as men condemned to death; for we have been made a spectacle to the world, both to angels and to men. We are fools for Christ's sake, but you are wise in Christ! We are weak, but you are strong! You are distinguished, but we are dishonored! To the present hour we both hunger and thirst, and we are poorly clothed, and beaten, and homeless. And we labor, working with our own hands. Being reviled, we bless; being persecuted, we endure; being defamed, we entreat. We have been made as the filth of the world, the off scouring of all things until now." (1 Corinthians 4:9-13)

Paul here describes the life of apostles as being "displayed" as a "spectacle" (Greek "theatre") to angels and men. God sets forth believers and especially leaders to show the world the values, actions and reactions of another kingdom. He points out that when believers suffer tribulation it is then that we most reveal the righteousness peace, joy and love that characterise those who dwell in the kingdom of God. When we are in difficulties we are declaring Christ and His effect on our lives more than at any other time. Leaders are not only preaching from the pulpit, whether they know it or not, they are preaching every day, and not only to people but to unseen powers and principalities as well.

Apostles: the pattern for spiritual leadership

The shaping of the apostles through the mentoring of Jesus Christ is one of the most remarkable facts of the New Testament. Christ demonstrates the breath-taking faith of God to take people who at first sight seem so unqualified.

They were mature men but relatively young.

It must be assumed that the twelve apostles were either the same age as Jesus or much younger. They were possibly in their early twenties when they were personally selected and there is no compelling reason to suppose they were older than 30 (Some have speculated that the apostles were at least 30 years of age because priests began their ministry at the age of 30 - see Numbers 4:3 – but Samuel and Jeremiah for example began their calling much younger). Despite their youth they were working men with families. Little is known about their private lives, but we know Peter was a fisherman and that he had a mother in law (Mark 1:30). Why so young? The answer is that some older believers often have already made their choices and shaped their minds. If this is true then the most critical period in the shaping of leaders is the first five years after their conversion. If believers are not drawn into ministry in their early years, it is possible that they will acquire a settled consciousness of disqualification. At the very least they may settle into a passive attitude to the ministry, believing that they are not qualified.

Obviously God also calls older people – Moses heard the call when he was 80 (and was full of energy and vision when he died at the age of 120). The challenge for us who are older is to keep laying our lives down on the altar so that God can renew our minds, thus keeping us open to fresh moves and waves of His Holy Spirit. The parable of the wine skins teaches us that the Holy Spirit needs freshly slain animal skins that are supple and able to change to the shape of the new wine. Believers must die daily and not allow time and force of habit to atrophy our sensitivity to the Holy Spirit.

When Jesus called Peter He immediately spoke into Peter's life that he was called to be an evangelist: *"Follow Me and I will make you fishers of men." (Matthew 4:18)*. This was not the end of the story for Peter, and it was three years later that Jesus spoke into his life again, and this time to make him into a pastor, a shepherd of the sheep: *"Feed My lambs," (John 21:15)*. When Jesus called James and John He did not say that they were to be fishers of men, but was silent on their calling. At the moment of their call they were *"mending their nets," (Matthew 4:21)*. This was perhaps indicative of their ministry of teaching the flock, of making a fine mesh for the net that would not let the fish be lost back into the sea.

When Paul was saved on the Damascus road, Jesus immediately commissioned him to carry the gospel to the nations:

> *"I have appeared to you for this purpose, to make you a minister and a witness of the things which you have seen, and of the things that I will yet reveal to you," (Acts 26:15-18)*

When people are converted and brought into the Kingdom of God, it is at that moment that their souls are very receptive to the gifts and calling of God on their lives. This does not mean that Church leaders should believe they can make all young converts into evangelists, pastors, teachers, prophets and apostles. It means that no hindrance or discouragement should be set in the path of God's people from entering fully into the active service of the King. This service will vary widely and all believers should be challenged and encouraged to discover and fulfil their calling right at the outset of their Christian lives.

They were imperfect men.

When Jesus chose the twelve they were far from perfect. Peter was a wobbly character, who could move from heights to depths within hours or even minutes. None of the disciples exhibited great faith when the storms arose, and they feared for their lives during the physical storms on the lake, and denied the Lord during the spiritual storm of the cross. Moreover most of the apostles were working men with little or no academic background. It is said of Peter and John that they were uneducated men (Acts 4:13). The cleverest disciples are not always the best! This does not mean that God cannot use intellectuals! God uses all the talents that are laid at His feet, and when Paul was saved, God used His powerful intellect to teach so many deep truths including vital insights into the Church and the Cross.

The point is that God does not wait for people to be perfect before He uses them. Rather He takes weak people and speaks into them things that were not in them before. Jesus called Simon bar Jonah a new name: Peter! This name means stone, and Peter became a living stone in the house of God by the voice of Jesus. Paul became a preacher by the voice of Jesus speaking deep into his spirit. God speaks prophetically into the hearts of believers to impart those qualities that are required. Older leaders and believers must believe that God can raise up another generation or their unbelief may stunt a rising generation.

Was Jesus taking a risk in choosing such young, inexperienced and weak men? The answer is not straightforward. He knew that they would falter and fail in the future, but He saw beyond that to their reshaping in brokenness to be vessels for Him. He made a choice that was supernatural. He spent a night in prayer before choosing these men (Luke 6:12) and thus embarked on the most daring act of faith. This is in itself an explanation of the command of Jesus:

> *"The harvest truly is plentiful, but the labourers are few. Pray therefore the Lord of the harvest to send out labourers into His harvest."* Matt 9:37-8.

It is vital that prayer be made that leads to daring faith in respect of the future of the Church.

The mystery of Judas.

It is a puzzling question: why did Jesus chose Judas? The Bible offers no special insights into the mind of the Lord in this matter. Judas is described in the Psalms as *"my own familiar friend." (Psalm 41:9)*. The word "familiar" is based on the Hebrew word "shalom" and indicates a measure of genuine friendship. Judas evidently received the same anointing of power as the others (Luke 9:1), although he had a fatal attraction to money and is described by John as a "thief" (John 12:6). The anointing of power had not made Judas a better man, just as Samson's anointing had not cured him of his sexual problems. The baptism of the Spirit is for the cleansing of hearts and is a deeper work than empowerment for ministry. It is a tragic mistake to direct men to seek power "on" their lives rather than purity through being made partakers of His life through the cross. There is no greater error than to separate the work of the Holy Spirit from the cross.

So why choose Judas? It is pure speculation but it is possible that Judas was given the best opportunity to get right with God. He had secret ambitions and sins which culminated in selling Jesus for 30 pieces of silver. But possibly that battle was one that had to be fought in the context of being a minister. The fact that Jesus foreknew what Judas would choose does not diminish the freedom of Judas to make his choice. No minister can avoid the fact that there are many battles that must be fought and won in the context of ministry. If God had chosen 12 perfect men then we would have to wait for men to be perfect before recognising them as leaders. But it will always be the case that ministers will face fierce temptations that can ruin their ministry and even damn their souls. Judas was a complex man who was both friendly to Jesus, and yet used Jesus for self-enrichment. Judas is the most solemn warning to all who are engaged in ministry. Paul himself recognised this same truth when he said:

"Thus I fight: not as one who beats the air. But I discipline my body and bring it into subjection, lest, when I have preached to others, I myself should become disqualified." (I Corinthians 9:26-27)

It is not only immorality that can destroy a man and a ministry, it is also the bitterness that poisons a heart through personal conflicts and divisions that take place in the Church. Temptations do not cease because we are leaders, rather they multiply.

The Central Call of Leaders/Apostles: the Revelation of Christ.

Spiritual leadership is based on the revelation of the person of Christ. When Peter confessed: *"You are the Christ, the Son of the living God,"* *(Matt 16:16)* he was reacting to the light that poured into his heart as he followed Christ. He had been chosen to receive this revelation, and it was this that equipped him to be the key leader in the New Testament Church. Every Church is built on the foundation of the revelation that lies in the heart of its leaders. The innermost sanctuary of any Church is the hearts and minds of its ministers. If the leaders have no personal experience of the Holy of Holies, then neither will the Church. Churches do not rise significantly above the spiritual level of their leaders, though individuals in the Church frequently do.

What leaders demonstrate by their character and preaching shapes the foundations of the Churches they build. When the pope wears special robes and carries a gold staff, those who look at him may legitimately but mistakenly conclude that this is a reflection of what Christ is like in heaven. In the same manner, every leadership team is declaring what they believe is the true representation of Christ in heaven. This is why apostles are so important; there must be a true representation of Christ at the heart of the Church.

Christ is the most amazing person, far greater than the wildest imaginations of human minds. The greatest fact about Him is that He is the true image of the Living God. There is no greater understanding of God than to know Jesus. He is God's chosen avenue of self-disclosure. This revelation of the person of Christ is God's method of shaping and commissioning apostles and there are several stages in this process.

Touching the centre:

""Who do men say that I, the Son of Man, am?" So they said:"
"You are the Messiah, the Son of the Living God."
(Matthew 16:13-14)

The first response of the disciples was to quote the rumours and speculations that were circulating about Jesus. It seems that there was an awareness that Jesus was at the very least a reincarnation of one of the greatest prophets ranging from Elijah, Jeremiah down to

John the Baptist who had only been dead a few months. There was already a wide spread belief that this Jesus had conquered death and was someone who had risen from the dead. The person of Jesus provoked comparison with three great men: John the Baptist, Elijah and Jeremiah.

"Some say you are John the Baptist." (Matthew 16:14)

John the Baptist had a very brief ministry. He began in the deserts as *"a voice crying in the wilderness." (Isaiah 40:3, Matt 3:1)*. This is certainly a strange place to begin a move of God. It is the opposite of common sense, which would direct a preacher into the large cities. John must have begun by witnessing to one or two individuals whom he met in the wastelands of Judea. The impact of that meeting provoked the people he witnessed to, to bring others to hear him. Soon crowds were flocking from Judea and all the region around the Jordan. John had nothing with which to attract the crowds other than a message from God. He did not preach healing or deliverance, and it is said of him that *"John performed no sign," (John 10:41)*. The ministry of John was to denounce sin and to lead the people to confess and repent. He used no "tricks" to gather crowds but relied on the power of the Holy Spirit to convict and persuade. This does not mean that the Holy Spirit does not lead people to build bridges to reach those who do not know God. Paul later preached in large cities and synagogues, adapting himself to those he was trying to reach:

> *"I have become all things to all men, that I might by all means save some,"*
> *(1 Corinthians 9:22)*

But John was given the ministry of shaking Israel by the power of his word, and bringing the nation to the possibility of repentance. John performed no signs and wonders, though it may be more accurate to say, that there was no emphasis on healing in his ministry. The miracle of lives changed was the fruit of his ministry, and as sinners found peace with God their blood pressure would have become

78

normal, tension would have disappeared, the grip of demonic strongholds would have been destroyed, and broken hearts would have been healed.

Some said that Jesus was John the Baptist risen from the dead. They thought that Jesus was just like John the Baptist but with the added dimension of having conquered death. Jesus like John led the nation to repentance by the power of His word and the holiness of His conduct.

"Others say Elijah." (Matthew 16:14)

There were others who affirmed that Jesus was more like Elijah. That great prophet had also led the nation to repentance, and John the Baptist himself had ministered in the spirit and power of Elijah (Luke 1:17). But Elijah had been a man of great signs and wonders. He had commanded the rain to cease, and the fire to fall. He had prayed for rain to return, and had raised the dead. Jesus also was a man of mighty miracles.

"Others say Jeremiah." (Matthew 16:14)

Jeremiah was the prophet of love. He had been the man who could scarcely speak without weeping. Like Jesus he had denounced sin in the temple and had wept over Jerusalem. The great mark of Jeremiah was his tears of love.

The point is that Jesus was so great a prophet that He incorporated in Himself all the prophets in their various emphases. He had the finely tuned hearing heart of Samuel. He attained greater spiritual heights than Moses. He had the fearless courage of Daniel. Jesus Christ had the quality of reminding the people of Israel of all their prophets. There was an abundance in His life and ministry that summed up the prophets and prophecies of the Old Testament and yet exceeded them all.

"You are the Messiah!" (Matthew 16:16)

The sense of the greatness of Jesus Christ impacted these 12 apostles. And then, in a moment of revelation, Peter uttered words that must have been forming in his heart. He confessed the astonishing truth that Messiah had indeed come at last. There are many aspects to this confession. On the one hand it was the confession that Jesus was the centre and culmination of all the ages *("the desire of all nations" Haggai 2:7)*. It was Messiah who would lead the nation of Israel to victory and overcome all their enemies (Daniel 2:44). Messiah would suffer and overcome sin and death (Daniel 9:24; 26 and Hosea 13:14). To Messiah would come all the Gentiles (Isaiah 60:1-7), and He would rule the world (Psalm 22:27-28). He would hold the title of Immanuel (Isaiah 7:14), the Mighty God, the Everlasting Father, the Prince of Peace (Isaiah 9:6). His kingdom would never pass away and would never cease to increase (Isaiah 9:7). It was the recognition that Jesus was the key to all humanity and the most important person who would ever live on planet earth. This was the longing of the human race from the garden of Eden (Genesis 3:15). It was the longing of Abraham (Genesis 22:18), the vision of Jacob (Genesis 49:10) and prophesied by Moses (Deuteronomy 18:15-19). He was prophesied by all the prophets from Moses to Malachi (Malachi 3:1), foreseen by Job (Job 19:25) and even foreseen by Balaam (Numbers 24:17-19).

On the other hand, it was the most incongruous setting. Important things happened in palaces didn't they? Kings commanding armies are the great movers and shakers of history aren't they? But here was a penniless carpenter, an itinerant preacher, talking privately to 12 unimportant men, of whom three were fishermen and one had been a corrupt tax official. It was only incongruous to worldly men, but to God it was exactly right. The moment when a human being recognises that Jesus is the Messiah is the most earth shaking thing that can ever happen. Christ has not come to take over governments and command armies of earth. He has come to breathe into the darkened and tired hearts of men and women the amazing truth of who God is. Messiah changes people from the inside.

Conclusion

The simplest fact of the Bible is that God stepped forth onto the stage of human history and revealed Himself through His Son Jesus, who is the Messiah and God in human form. Knowing that He is the Messiah is the threshold of the discovery of God and the means by which we have eternal life.

> *"These are written that you may believe that Jesus is the Christ, the Son of God, and that believing you may have life in His name." (John 20:31)*

Apostolic leadership is not built on amazing human abilities. Apostles have encountered Jesus the Messiah and have become gripped with the wonder of His personality, and are equipped and inspired by God to share their discoveries to a dying world.

CHAPTER 5

APOSTLES AND REVELATION

The greatest revelation is that the man born in Bethlehem is Jesus the Messiah, and God in human form. Jesus is the Son of God and God the Son. This is not a matter of argument, or logical deduction, but a simple fact of the Godhead that is revealed. This is the most foundational revelation of all and is the basis of all that can ever be revealed to a human being about the heart of God. God's power and intelligence are revealed in part through the created world. God's holiness is made known in part through the inner conscience that demands righteousness and justice. But the fullness of God's character and heart are only known through Jesus.

When a person recognises that Jesus is the Messiah he has passed into the key realm of God's self-disclosure. God wants to be known and understood, and for this He sent His Son. The crowds of believers who surrounded Jesus were conscious of His uniqueness, but God wanted to share deeper things about Himself, and for this He needs men who will follow on and become witnesses of the treasures that lie hidden in the Godhead. Every minister is a witness of Christ whether he is conscious of this fact or not. For example, when a leader becomes anxious about the Church and passes into a depressed state, the onlookers will unconsciously believe that Christ is worried. Or if a leader is one who loves riches and high living, this will be the way that Christ is assumed to be. The truth is that the Church needs ministers who have become witnesses of the hidden depths of the character of Christ. Such ministers will be purified from worry, the love of money and other vain distractions.

Level 1: conversion.

The apostles were witnesses of Christ in different levels. Firstly, they experienced the wonder of conversion. The accounts indicate that it was their encounter with Jesus that arrested them. Andrew was gripped with the consciousness of the greatness of Jesus from the first meeting described in John 1:35-40. His reaction was to find Peter and declare: *"We have found the Messiah" (John 1:41)*. Later Jesus found them and called them from fishing to follow Him (Mark 1:16-17). Their instant reaction was to leave all and follow Him. The impact of Jesus was breath-taking and instant.

Of all the apostles, the conversion of Matthew is the most stunning. Matthew was not a country bumpkin who could be accused of gullibility. He was a tax collector, which meant that he was a shrewd operator, taking advantage of both the tax payers and the Roman authorities. Tax collectors were so corrupt that they were grouped with prostitutes as the worst sinners of their day (Luke 15:1). Their sin included their betrayal of their nation Israel through collaboration with the Romans. Matthew was also an educated man which can be deduced from reading his gospel. Yet when he was suddenly confronted with Jesus something happened that changed his life in an instant.

> *"After these things He went out and saw a tax collector named Levi (Matthew), sitting at the tax office. And He said to him, "Follow Me." So he left all, rose up, and followed Him." Luke 5:27-28.*

The only explanation for this is the instant consciousness of the greatness of Jesus. Was it the presence of God that could be sensed as He drew near? Was it the face of a man who had never sinned?

Looking into that face Matthew would have seen peace, serenity, authority and purity. Jesus had no pain of guilt and regret, he had no anxieties or worries. He had no fear of sickness, death or any power of darkness. Jesus was penniless but had nothing of the beggar about Him. He was dressed in the clothes of a working man, yet there was a dignity and majesty about Him that made Him different. As Matthew gazed into those eyes, perhaps the most stunning quality was His love, His grace, His lack of condemnation, His pity combined with strength and humility. At the same time there was the absence of superstition or religiosity. There was a joy and gladness, an eagerness and energy that indicated a deep sense of purpose and hope.

What Matthew saw was the opposite of his own life. He was aware of the appalling condition of his conscience, defiled through his shabby life style. In his heart was the guilt of many lies, and the moral weakness of a man who had sacrificed inner values on the altar of self-advancement. Matthew had lived for money. His eyes were veiled with lies, and his heart would have had to suppress the fear of sickness, poverty, death, judgment and hell. In the first century, death was a constant reality with wars, brutal merciless government, along with few cures or treatments for the maladies of the human race. When Matthew saw Jesus he was presented with a choice: to stay the same or to seize the opportunity and follow Jesus. He would have instantly known that he could not have both. Luke records that Matthew did three things: first he left all. That was a decision of the heart, to forsake his life style whatever the cost. Second, he rose up. That indicates the resurgence of hope and the faith that there was a better world to live for. Third, he followed Him. This was the expression of a faith that surrendered the future to Jesus Christ. It was an act of incredible abandon for one with such a background of moral weakness. All the apostles were different but all of them were gripped with the sense of this man filling all the aching void of human life. Christ gave them certainty, not by words and arguments, but by the touch of the divine in human form.

Level 2. Witnesses of His teaching.

The apostles were privileged to hear Him preach and teach. The Bible records that they had limited understanding but were given deeper insights in private conversation (Mark 4:10). Jesus said that it was given to them

> *"to know the mystery of the kingdom of God; but to those who are outside, all things come in parables." (Mark 4:11).*

This pattern of giving special insights to the apostles continued right to the end, culminating in the upper room when He washed their feet and taught them about the Holy Spirit (John chapters 13-17). It continued through the resurrection until the day He ascended. The apostles were taught by Jesus. They were given the same teaching as the crowds, but were given deeper insights and keys to understanding the kingdom of God.

The apostles and other writers like Luke and Mark who were not apostles completed the canon of scripture, and there is no further teaching or revelation to add to it, but there is the need to freshly grasp the teaching of Christ along with its implications. It is far beyond the scope of a few paragraphs to summarise the teachings of Jesus (that will have to be the subject of another book!) Nevertheless it is vital to reflect on what the essential teaching of Jesus was.

1. The sermon on the Mount (Matthew 5-7) and John 3. These two sections of the New Testament are the "opening words" of Jesus in His teaching ministry. The first words that Jesus preached were *"repent for the kingdom of heaven is at hand (Matt 4:17).* In His first teaching He taught the moral excellence of

the kingdom, surpassing the righteousness of the scribes and Pharisees (Matt 5:20). He describes the spiritual centre of the kingdom: a relationship in prayer with God as Father (Matt 6:9). He describes the rock like foundation of the kingdom that will stand on the stormiest day of human history – the day of judgement (Matt 7:24-25). He also teaches that none of this is attainable without a new birth from above (John 3:5).

2. The parables of the kingdom (Matthew 13, Mark 4, John 15). In the parables Jesus taught that the Christian life is not a work to be done, but a plant to be cultivated in anticipation of reaping a great harvest. Christians are to attend to the atmosphere of their hearts, and treasure the word of the kingdom allowing it to grow without the weeds of worry and lust, or the hard ground of indifference and superficiality. If we will make room for the seed, it will grow of itself into the fullness of the life that God desires.

3. The parable of the Father's heart (Luke 15). This parable stands in sublime declaration of the love of the Father that lies behind the gospel as its driving force. This is the subject of the teaching of Jesus in John's gospel, that God is essentially a Father, who loves the world and sent His Son to redeem it.

4. The future return of Christ to judge the nations (Matthew 24-25). Jesus taught that Israel would be scattered, but would ultimately be re gathered at the end of history. There would be earthquakes and plagues shaking the world before His return, but that the gospel will be preached in every people group. The day of judgment would be without partiality, and judgment will begin with the house of God.

5. The Holy Spirit was promised as the comforter who would come after Christ's passion to empower His followers through the power of indwelling. The Holy Spirit would

grant His followers gifts and knowledge to witness to the reality of Christ. (John 14-17).

6. The kingdom of God is built on different principles to the world. His followers must forgive and be merciful (Matthew 18). His followers must receive one another as little children, and prefer one another, washing each other's feet and living a life of selfless love and service (John 13).

7. The religious hypocrisy of the Pharisees was a common human failing which is a deadly poison that must be avoided at all costs (Matthew 23). Insincerity in preaching produces "hollow men and women" whose lives contradict Christian ideals.

Level 3 Witnesses of His power.

The apostles saw Jesus do miracles including the healing of all kinds of diseases, raising the dead and the deliverance of severely troubled souls. They saw Him multiply loaves and fishes, calm storms and walk on water. The apostles would have believed that everything was possible to the one who believed in Jesus.

Level 4 Witnesses that Jesus is the Messiah.

This understanding of the identity of Christ was dawning from their first encounters, and was vocalised at key moments, most notably when Peter made his declaration that Jesus was more than a prophet, more than one risen from the dead: Jesus is the Messiah.

Level 5 Witnesses of His character.

Spiritual leaders must pass through these levels of being witnesses of Christ. They must be converted, they must know the teaching, the power, and the identity of Christ. But this is only the beginning. The true test of spiritual leadership is in knowing what Jesus is like as a person, what moves Him, what pleases or displeases Him: they must know His heart. Of all the dimensions of spiritual leadership this is the most important. Some leaders can teach, do miracles and practice deliverance ministry and yet not be aware of the deep currents that flow in the heart of God. This level of knowing Jesus is immeasurable, and no matter how far we may progress in knowing Him, we are still only paddling in the shallows of His greatness.

Jesus lifted the veil on His character at three key moments and He took with Him His three main leaders Peter, James and John, who were to lead the Church after His ascension into heaven.

The Raising of Jairus's Daughter (Mark 5:21-43)

This event shows us that the secret of true power is love. It came at the end of an incredibly busy phase of powerful ministry by Jesus. He had taught by Lake Galilee, crossed the lake, delivered the Gadarene, re-crossed the lake to be met by huge crowds, and amongst them He had received Jairus's earnest request to come and heal his dying daughter. The Lord had not hesitated, but had immediately followed Jairus.

On their way, a woman with a haemorrhage lasting 12 years had touched Him. She had done this secretly as if she believed she could 'pick His pocket' and take away her healing without Him noticing. The reason for this was that she knew the Law, which declared that anyone touching a person defiled with blood would instantly become unclean. No Pharisee would have allowed her to approach him. Her tragedy was that her sickness separated her from all touch and affection. How true this is of sin - that by it our hearts become strangers to the inner awareness of God's love. The wonder of the whole event is that, when she was discovered, she heard the Lord's voice calling out, not with disgust or condemnation, but with love and kindness. His voice drew confession from her lips and she told Him everything in a few words. How great her delight and wonder, when she heard the blessed words of adoption from His lips:

> *"Daughter, your faith has made you well. Go in peace and be healed of your affliction."* (Mark 5:34)

And then the news came to Jairus: *"Your daughter is dead."* This was met by the quiet confidence of the Lord: *"Only believe".* The sight of the mourners was an offence to Jesus, knowing their hypocrisy, but this did not stop Him from seeking to win them. He declared the wonderful truth of faith, that death is not the cessation of life; it is only a temporary rest in the bosom of the Father at the end of life's day, whether that day be long or short. Death is sleep, and is just the prelude to the morning, when the dead in Christ shall awake and arise. But the mourners had no faith in God's word, which often spoke of death as sleep - as when *"David slept (or rested) with his fathers" (1 Kings 2:10).*

So Jesus drove the mourners away, and took the girl's parents and the three apostles in with Him. There He again defied the Law of uncleanness, which said that He could not touch a dead body without defilement. He took the girl by the hand and said the words: *"Talitha Cumi"*, which means, *"My little pet lamb, I say to you, arise."* (Mark 5:41).

Here lie foundational principles of Church life; chiefly, that power does not lie in great noise, but in tender love. But further to this, that power lies in a word from God, spoken in a whisper. True leaders must lead the flock to such a Saviour, for the tender lambs will not open to anyone else. God has not called leaders simply to lead for the sake of leading! They are called to lead men and women to the fountains of living waters.

The Transfiguration *(Mark 9:2-10)*

Here was a truly remarkable revelation. Christ led them up the mountain, and there His form was changed, and they saw unspeakable glory. They saw beyond the veil of Christ's human flesh into the glory of heaven itself - seeing even the glorified Moses and Elijah. Finally they heard the voice of the Father Himself speaking directly and audibly.

Here in this simple and direct confrontation with the invisible Kingdom of God lie the foundations of that kingdom. The first is in the brightness of the holiness and the glory. They witnessed a light and a purity, such as none on earth could ever equal, and this was the inner life of Christ shining through. All leaders must have some awareness of glory, of surpassing holiness. Without this they will falter in the face of the surpassing evil that is in the world. They will not keep going unless they know there is a sinless One, who can never be defiled, and who has lived in this world without defilement. His Church is glorious, because she is bone of His bone, flesh of His flesh, partaking of His glory by His indwelling in our hearts through the person of the Holy Spirit. The early Church did not have great programmes or detailed strategies. Their leaders were imprisoned, persecuted and executed - quite a pattern to follow! But through all the conflict came the blazing awareness of the reality of the unseen Christ glorified at the right hand of the Father. It is small wonder that Stephen's face also shone like that of an angel while beholding the glory of God, and Jesus standing at God's right hand (Acts 7:55-56).

The knowledge of glory is to know that which is overwhelming. When a man is in communion with God there will be moments when He is conscious of a Presence that is more than he is able to bear. The glory is the outshining of God's person which radiates holiness and love. As we receive the waves of this glory we are changed, our character is purified, and there is an impartation of love into our souls. The key to spiritual growth is to gaze on Christ:

"We all, with unveiled face, beholding as in a mirror the glory of the Lord, are being transformed into the same image from glory to glory, just as by the Spirit of the Lord." 2 Corinthians 3:18.

The words of the Father to the three apostles are also an open window into the Godhead. The simple declaration was: *"This is My beloved Son, hear him."* (Mark 9:7). This revealed to them what it means to be loved. The Church is to be a declaration to the world of what it is to be loved by God.

Insecurity is the most common cause of strain in a leader. A leader must know what it is to be loved by God. He will then not be filled with fears and anxieties. This is a revolutionary state of being, since the world does not know what it is like to be loved through and through, till there are no more fears and worries, till there is no more condemnation. The Bible tells us that Jesus is in the "bosom of the Father" (John 1:18). This indicates that Jesus is in the heart of God and in the loving embrace of the Father. That is the key to the healing of the soul and the maintaining of a healthy mind.

The Agony in Gethsemane (Mark 14:32-42)

In Gethsemane, the Lord again took only Peter, James and John with Him to witness the awful agony that came on His soul there in the garden.

Leaders must in some degree witness the soul-rending agony that crushed the soul of the Lord Jesus in the garden. This agony was the experience of the Son of Man, i.e. of Christ in His manhood. It is significantly absent from John's Gospel, which concentrates on Christ as the Son of God, and does not describe the temptations in the wilderness. This does not mean that Christ was a divided personality, sometimes acting as God and sometimes as man. Christ was fully human and fully divine, and the love of God that burned in His heart caused the Man Christ Jesus to agonise over human sin with a sorrow that brought Him to the gates of death.

Such a physical state is quite rare and yet is not unknown in human hearts. The grief of bereavement has claimed people's lives, and Christ, there in the garden, declared that the sorrow He bore was

91

crushing Him nearly to death. He prayed for strength, for he wanted to prevail and persevere to the cross so that He might die not only of a broken heart, but also as the sacrifice for the sins of the whole world.

People guess at God's nature, but no-one really knows either the Father or the Son unless they are revealed. The Church is founded on the revelation of God in Christ. Jesus declared this to Peter, when he saw in a flash the truth beyond flesh and blood that the Son of God was here. Jesus said that He would build His Church on this revelation. He surely did not mean that He would build His Church on the mere doctrine of Christ's divinity, but that He would build it on the revelation to human hearts of Christ's true nature. This is apostolic mission and the mission of the whole Church - to know Him, and to declare Him in the midst of the Church, and also to a dying world, so that the invisible God might be fully known throughout the length and breadth of the earth.

This definition of apostolic ministry includes all the main ministries of the Church that operate in some measure of leadership in the Church. Prophets, evangelists, pastors and teachers must all, to some degree, be people who declare the unseen riches of Christ.

Level 6 Witnesses of the cross.

The greatest revelation of God in all eternity took place on planet earth when the son of God was crucified. That Christ was the Messiah is the greatest fact of human history. His words are the most important words ever spoken. His death is the most important event, and it is at once the most terrible sin of the human race, and the most wonderful declaration of the heart of God. Paradoxically the apostles were all absent from this moment, except for John. The women persisted to the end, though to be fair it may well have been that the apostles ran the greater danger of arrest and death. The apostles were to become true witnesses of the cross but only after the coming of the Holy Spirit: this will be examined later in chapter 7

Conclusion: the power of Revelation.

Paul prayed for the Ephesian believers:

> *"That the God of our Lord Jesus Christ, the Father of glory, may give you the spirit of wisdom and revelation in the knowledge of Him, the eyes of your understanding being enlightened; that you may know what is the hope of His calling, what are the riches of the glory of His inheritance in the saints, and what is the exceeding greatness of His power toward us who believe, according to the working of His mighty power which He worked in Christ when He raised Him from the dead and seated Him at His right hand in the heavenly places, far above all principality and power and might and dominion, and every name that is named, not only in this age but also in that which is to come. And He put all things under His feet, and gave Him to be head over all things to the church, which is His body, the fullness of Him who fills all in all." (Ephesians 1:17-23)*

Christ is in His people in matchless authority, incredible glory and limitless power and love. May God open our eyes to what He has already put within us by Christ in us, the hope of glory.

CHAPTER 6

APOSTLES AND BROKENNESS

The apostles were taught by Jesus as He preached and ministered. They would also have been conscious of the greatness of Jesus and this must have filled them with hope that they in their turn might receive a similar anointing. But as their years following Jesus went by, the apostles would have been keenly aware of the supreme greatness of Jesus and the spiritual poverty of their own hearts. Jesus led them through these years to teach them these two truths. Unless both truths are grasped believers are not able to realise the fullness of His grace.

The grace of Christ abounds in the lives of those who know their own inability to be like Him. This lesson came through the words of Jesus when He said "Blessed are the poor in spirit, for theirs is the kingdom of heaven." (Matthew 5:3). But this lesson came strongest through the events through which they passed. When the apostles came to the day of Pentecost, their faith in Him was soaring, and their faith in themselves had completely vanished. This is the mark of broken men and women, and it is a vital foundation for spiritual leadership.

Brokenness may seem at first sight to be negative, since a broken watch or camera is of no use. But in the spiritual world, brokenness refers to the right estimation of oneself and an ability to humble oneself quickly and without fuss. It includes the ability to confess one's faults, the ability to take a humble path, to suffer, to serve, to forgive and to love.

The path to brokenness.

The apostles were led by the Lord both to receive the fullness of the Holy Spirit and to see that fullness fully released. Often the power is not released because the vessel is not broken. What happened on the day of Pentecost was a combination of extraordinary power combined with deep brokenness.

Stages in the journey of brokenness.

Stage 1. The emptiness of power.

Very early in their walk with the Lord the apostles received power to cast out all demons and heal all diseases (Matthew 10:1 and Luke 9:1). This power together with the ministry of apostleship was also given to Judas. This power was given some three years before Pentecost, and did not improve the character of the disciples. At first sight it may seem strange to think of this power as a lesson in brokenness. The apostles had to learn that success and power in their ministry did not mean a better quality of life. This is the paradox of brokenness: the heart must begin to thirst for power to live, for the power that makes us better people. The apostles were probably eager for power to do miracles. But they quickly had to learn that such power cannot ultimately satisfy either God or man. This in no way minimises the anointing that Jesus gives His followers, but it puts it in the context of a broken vessel through which the glory and beauty of Christ are to shine through.

Just imagine for a moment the thanks that the apostles would have received through the exercise of this power. They would have been honoured by the crowds, and received in homes as great men. They might have been offered money in appreciation for their ministry, and given their sacrificial life style, they would arguably have been justified in receiving gifts. But these accolades and honours are a snare and can bring out carnal attitudes such as pride and self-importance. Ministers need to be broken or power will ruin them.

Stage 2. The fear of death.

Jesus took the disciples into moments of danger and vulnerability. (Mark 4:36-41). The disciples feared for their lives as they faced apparently certain death. The storm raged around them, but a deeper storm was raging in their hearts. They were afraid to die. When Jesus said "How is it that you have no faith?" (Mark 4:40) he was indicating that they had no faith in the face of death. Their beliefs were shredded by the force of reality.

In late 1735 John Wesley was aboard a ship sailing from England to the American colonists in Savannah, Georgia. The weather turned bad and the ship was in danger of sinking. Wesley, the chaplain of the vessel was afraid to die. He was aware of a group of German Moravians who were also on their way to preach the gospel in America. They were not afraid of the storm at all and sang quietly in great serenity. Later Wesley asked the Moravian leader about their calm. The Moravians' leader asked him whether he, Wesley, had faith in Christ. Wesley assured him he did, but later wrote in his journal "I fear they were vain words." This set Wesley on course to discovering the reality of Christ in 1738.

Faith in the face of death is not a natural quality, though some men do have great courage. God shows us our weakness so that in the darkest hour light may arise.

Stage 3. Kingdom values.

In Mark 10:13-14 some women approached Jesus with little children. The apostles completely misread the heart of the Lord and blocked their access to Him. The apostles had to learn that their values were not consistent with the kingdom of God. In the kingdom of men strength is important, children are kept well away, but in the kingdom of God the weak and vulnerable are of central importance. Love is the foundation while gentleness and meekness are key qualities. The apostles had to learn the ways of agape love. It is remarkable that this is one of the rare occasions when the Lord was "displeased" with his apostles. It is rare to see Jesus angry in the gospel accounts, and it is very rare to see him angry with his own followers. This indicates that their failure was of the deepest quality. What motivated the apostles to reject children? Was it a sense of their own self-importance? The rebuke of the Lord is a precious ointment for those who are humble enough to receive it. Often this rebuke comes through circumstances where our values are exposed. It is possible to think the rebuke was easier to swallow for the apostles, but resentment can arise in any heart unless we quickly and deeply acknowledge our spiritual weakness.

Stage 4. Understanding the mysteries.

The apostles were not intellectual giants and were capable of completely misunderstanding the Lord as in Mark 8:15-17. The Lord had his twelve on board a boat again. As they bobbed up and down on the waves, it may be that they wondered what lessons on the instability of their world they were about to learn this time. On the voyage across the lake the Lord told them to beware of the leaven of the Pharisees and the leaven of Herod

(Mark 8:15). The apostles reflected on the possible meaning of this mysterious statement and concluded that He was rebuking them for not bringing bread to eat. Their mistake is breath-taking and many readers of the gospels will smile, presuming that they are sharper than the apostles. But the truth is that all human beings frequently and regularly misunderstand the Lord. The Lord rebuked His disciples with stinging words that made them aware of the hardness of their hearts and the slowness of their spiritual acumen.

"Do you not yet perceive nor understand? Is your heart still hardened? Having eyes, do you not see? And having ears, do you not hear? And do you not remember?" (Mark 8:17-18)

God does not build his kingdom on clever men, but on broken people, who have so faced their ignorance that they are humble enough to receive instruction and understanding from the Lord. The worst quality in any leader is the inability to admit being wrong.

Stage 5. Learning to consider others better than ourselves.

In Mark 9:33-4 the Lord asked the apostles what they had been arguing about in the way. Their silence is eloquent, and none dared raise the matter in His presence, for they had been arguing about who was to be the greatest among them. One can imagine their conversation.

Peter: "Well I have received the keys of the kingdom!"
John: "Yes but I understand Him best and am closest to Him."
Matthew: "That's all very well, but neither of you have much experience of the real world (business). And Peter made such a fool of himself trying to show off by walking on the water!"
Simon the Zealot: "But what do you all know about politics? If

we are to make an impact on the world we will need men of experience from the halls of power."

Thomas: "You are all too impulsive, we need a man of caution and prudence to lead the movement."

Simmering beneath the surface was their pride, ambition and self-importance. Jesus took a little child, weak and vulnerable, out of its depth in the adult world, inexperienced and frail, trusting and open. Jesus taught them that our attitude must not be self-important but esteeming others better and greater. The kingdom is not for the strong but for the meek. Leaders are often strong men who will find themselves in conflict with one another. It is vital that in times of such bitter conflict we step back and realise how vain we sound to the Lord. It is His will that we die to self and take the lowest place.

Stage 6. Tongue-tied in prayer.

In Mark 14:37-40 Jesus took His three closest leaders and asked them to watch while He prayed. The result was that they fell soundly asleep. The hour was dark and the danger real. The effect on their spirits was to make them lose focus and allow sleep to steal over them. No one can blame them, and hardly ever do we hear of people repenting of the sin of prayerlessness. Of all the lessons in brokenness, this is perhaps the most important. Ministers too easily become spiritually dry and give up praying. It is easy to substitute reaching out to God with dusty rituals of praying through lists. Prayer is the most revealing exercise of the soul, and few will claim greatness in this area. Every spiritual leader who is going deeper with God must have the ability to shut himself up with the Lord and seek His face. This is not a secondary spiritual quality of leadership, but an essential and foundational one. Our need of the Holy Spirit is never more keenly felt than when we are alone praying.

Our deepest brokenness is before the throne of God, as we reach out to understand and commune with the eternal God. It is in such moments that our souls are forced to their deepest honesty before God. Human beings can pretend and bluff their way through many things, but our masks nearly always slip when we are praying. Even children can tell when someone is insincere, and insincerity in prayer is a poison. Of all the trials they passed through, as the apostles reflected on their prayer life, they would have realised they were not just slow learners, they were completely ineffective and powerless. If someone had said that the future of the Church rested on their prayers, they would have either laughed in derision or sunk in despair. The apostles could not pray, and this consciousness was the vital antechamber to the discovery of the incredible power centre of the kingdom. It is in our weakest moments that we are on the verge of the greatest discoveries in the kingdom of God. Sometimes when we feel furthest from our goals, we are actually nearing the moment of their most stunning fulfilment. If you are feeling weak and are passing through deep trials, take heart, for you are in the very forecourts of eternity.

Peter: a lesson in brokenness.

Among the twelve Peter was the most vocal and the most spontaneous. He was an extrovert and wore his heart on his sleeve. There are four occasions when we see Peter learning the hard way that he was completely powerless and unable of himself to contribute to the kingdom of God.

Jesus teaches Peter how to fish.

"So it was, as the multitude pressed about Him to hear the word of God, that He stood by the Lake of Gennesaret, and saw two boats standing by

the lake; but the fishermen had gone from them and were washing their nets. Then He got into one of the boats, which was Simon's, and asked him to put out a little from the land. And He sat down and taught the multitudes from the boat. When He had stopped speaking, He said to Simon, "Launch out into the deep and let down your nets for a catch." But Simon answered and said to Him, "Master, we have toiled all night and caught nothing; nevertheless at Your word I will let down the net." And when they had done this, they caught a great number of fish, and their net was breaking. So they signalled to their partners in the other boat to come and help them. And they came and filled both the boats, so that they began to sink. When Simon Peter saw it, he fell down at Jesus' knees, saying, "Depart from me, for I am a sinful man, O Lord!" For he and all who were with him were astonished at the catch of fish which they had taken; and so also were James and John, the sons of Zebedee, who were partners with Simon. And Jesus said to Simon, "Do not be afraid. From now on you will catch men. So when they had brought their boats to land, they forsook all and followed Him." (Luke 5:1-11).

Jesus told Peter to let down his nets to catch fish. Peter's reaction is one of unbelief. He tells Jesus that he has been fishing the whole night and has caught nothing. The implication is that Jesus is mistaken in His instruction. There is a depth of patronising disdain in the word "nevertheless" (verse 5). Peter implies that Jesus may know much about spiritual matters but does not understand how to fish. When their nets are filled to the point that the boats are sinking Peter realises how foolish he has been. Peter's confession that he is a sinful man is a realisation of his own wickedness in thinking so highly of himself and so low of Jesus. This was the second time that Peter abandoned fishing, and it was not the last. In John 21 Peter again resorts to fishing and once more toils all night in fruitless labour. Once more it is the Lord who knows more about fishing than Peter. Peter had to learn that Jesus is Lord of all. Peter's confession "I am a sinful man" kneeling in front of Jesus is the cry of a broken man.

Peter: angel or demon?

On a more solemn level Peter was on one occasion a channel for the thoughts of Satan moments after receiving a revelation from God. In Matthew 16:16 Peter makes the great confession that Jesus is the Messiah. In response Jesus gives Peter the revelation that the He will build His Church on the rock of the revelation of Himself. Then Jesus promised to give to Peter the keys of the kingdom. This promise was to Peter alone. The Greek indicates that Jesus spoke to Peter using the second person singular, ("thee" in Old English). Peter must have felt exultant at these fast moving exchanges. He must have felt the rush of wonderment at the consciousness that Jesus was the Messiah. He would then have been amazed that he was singled out to receive the mysterious honour of holding the keys of the kingdom. Peter was soaring in elation at his spiritual achievements. But then comes an abrupt change of mood as Jesus begins to explain that He will be betrayed in Jerusalem and be killed and rise again the third day. Peter was emboldened by his success and rebuked Jesus. He said to Jesus:

> *"Pity thyself" (Matthew 16:22 KJV margin), "Far be it from You Lord; this shall not happen to You" (NKJV).*

The Lord turned to Peter with the severest rebuke:

> *"Get behind Me, Satan! You are an offense to Me, for you are not mindful of the things of God, but the things of men." Then Jesus said to His disciples, "If anyone desires to come after Me, let him deny himself, and take up his cross, and follow Me. For whoever desires to save his life will lose it, but whoever loses his life for My sake will find it. For what profit is it to a man if he gains the whole world, and loses his own soul? Or what will a man give in exchange for his soul?"" Matthew 16:23-26.*

What was so wrong with Peter's words to Jesus "pity thyself"? The answer lies in the tragedy of a merely sentimental response to the human condition. Our response to the heartbreak of evil is to wish it away. But Jesus could see that the only response to the misery of sin was to break the power of evil through the sacrifice of Calvary. Peter had not the slightest clue either about the darkness of the human soul, nor of the need for a redeeming sacrifice that would heal the deepest ills which afflict people. When Jesus rebuked Peter, He also rebuked every diluted form of Christianity that offers a soothing but ineffective cure to the open sore of sin. Jeremiah said of the false prophets:

"For they have healed the hurt of the daughter of My people slightly, Saying, "Peace, peace!" When there is no peace." (Jeremiah 8:11)

Peter had to learn that there are elements of our human response that are Satanic. (Self-pity, the feeling of being a victim, is one of the most common emotions encouraged in our present culture, on occasions even by Christians). Once human beings begin to adapt the Christian message, it loses its power. Christianity without a cross is a Satanic invention.

Some may flinch at this assessment, but that may because of the use of the word "Satan". Many will think of demons and witches when this word is used. But the Bible presents a different and more subtle perception of that arch enemy of the human race. If Satan were allowed to give a lecture to the assembled professors of the most distinguished universities, he would not appear with horns and a trident in his hand. He would be dressed in a suit, and would so flatter and engage the intelligence of his audience that at the end of his address they would give him a standing ovation. Genesis 3:1 describes him as the most cunning of all the creatures that God made. The Hebrew word for "cunning" can also be translated "subtle, shrewd, sly, sensible." Peter learned that he could be a channel for ideas that were completely out of step with the wisdom of God. Satan is in his most dangerous disguise when clothed in religious and moral wisdom that sidesteps the cross. It is mere speculation, but it is probable that when Jesus confronted Satan in the temptations in the wilderness and finally on Calvary, Satan was filled with the deepest dread, knowing he was battling the incorruptible God in human form.

Touching the depths.

Peter's deepest test came during the trial of Jesus. Peter had vowed never to deny Jesus and had expressed his determination to die rather than disown his Lord. Jesus had warned Peter that he was about to face the deepest trial of his spiritual life.

> *"And the Lord said, "Simon, Simon! Indeed, Satan has asked for you, that he may sift you as wheat. "But I have prayed for you, that your faith should not fail; and when you have returned to Me, strengthen your brethren." But he said to Him, "Lord, I am ready to go with You, both to prison and to death." Then He said, "I tell you, Peter, the rooster shall not crow this day before you will deny three times that you know Me." Luke 22:31-34.*

Peter's devotion was well intentioned but not strong enough to stand in the face of the threat of death. Peter's courage vanished at the question of a young woman who recognized him from his accent. Three times she insisted he was one of Jesus' disciples. Three times Peter denied the Lord and on the third time he cursed and swore that he did not know Jesus (Mark 14:71). Perhaps he was trying to prove by the manner of his speech that he was not a follower of Christ. Whom did he curse? What did he swear? His language was profane and persuaded the accusers that he was not a follower of Jesus. Then the cock crew and the enormity of what he had done hit Peter. Luke tells us that Jesus caught his eye across the courtyard (Luke 22:61). It must have been a look of love thrown as a lifebuoy to save a drowning man. The love of Christ would have melted Peter's heart and in that moment something broke deep in his life. Peter's innermost being split open and he wept and wept. Such depths of brokenness are precarious moments and God guides us into them and through them. Peter was a prepared vessel. Three days later the angels gave the message to the women at the tomb to *"go and tell his disciples – and Peter – that He is going before you into Galilee"* (Mark 16:7). Luke tells us that Jesus appeared privately to Peter (Luke 24:34). These personal words and touches from the Lord were essential for Peter's healing, and they are equally essential in our lives. God breaks open our hearts, and pours in healing grace.

Peter: broken, healed and ready.

The last resurrection appearance to Peter is described in John 21. Here Jesus renews His call to Peter and redirects his ministry to caring for the flock. At first Jesus had called him to be an evangelist. Now he is to be a shepherd. Jesus asks Peter the searching question "Do you love me with agape love?" John 21:15. Peter's reaction had lost the bluster and the self-confidence. He is unable to make an absolute declaration of love for Jesus. He uses the word "phileo" in his response indicating that he is his friend (John 21:15;16 Living Bible). Kenneth Taylor translates this conversation as follows:

> *"Simon, son of John, do you love Me more than these others?"*
> *"Yes," Peter replied, "You know I am your friend."*
> *"Then feed my lambs," Jesus told him.*
> *Jesus repeated the question: "Simon, son of John, do you really love Me?"*
> *"Yes, Lord," Peter said, "You know I am your friend."*
> *"Then take care of My sheep," Jesus said.*
> *Once more He asked him, "Simon, son of John, are you even my friend?"*
> *Peter was grieved at the way Jesus asked the question this third time. "Lord, You know my heart; You know I am," he said.*
> *Jesus said, "Then feed My little sheep." John 21:15-17 Living Bible.*

Peter was now ready to receive the Holy Spirit and rely on Him. For many believers the lessons in brokenness come after the Holy Spirit is received. But whether before or after, the lessons are vital so that we may trust in Christ alone.

Peter had learned that his level of commitment was not the foundation of his Christian life. The faithfulness and love of Jesus are the rock on which we build. Being broken in His hands involves deep honesty of heart, a willingness to repent quickly and believe in His justifying love. It is precisely these qualities that made Peter such a great man of God.

Conclusion:

The power of broken vessels filled with the Holy Spirit.

The transformation of the apostles on the day of Pentecost is evident from the account in the book of Acts. The apostles had a vibrant spiritual life and they dedicated themselves to prayer (Acts 6:4). They were bold and fearless in the face of death (Acts 4:18-19). Their understanding of spiritual things was consistently deep and insightful (Acts 2:14-36). They had greater power than ever (Acts 5:15) but they knew this power was not from them (Acts 3:12). They had agape love and shared all things (Acts 2:44) and were able to remain united through difficult and divisive issues (Acts 15). This does not mean that they were perfect, and their brokenness had to be renewed and deepened to ensure that the power of God still rested on them (2 Corinthians 12:9-10). Jesus invested three and a half years in training these men, and His initial choice was not based on their superior intellectual strength but on their readiness to humble themselves quickly and believe in His forgiveness and move on. Perhaps the greatest achievement of His years of ministry was the eleven apostles: men emptied of self and full of God.

CHAPTER 7

APOSTLES: WITNESSES OF THE CROSS

Ministers of Christ and Him Crucified - 1 Corinthians 2:2.

When Paul declared his determination to preach nothing but Christ and Him crucified, it was in the context of his letter of correction to the Corinthian Church. The leaders in Corinth must have been embarrassed because it would have exposed the central cause of the moral and doctrinal disasters that were afflicting them: their failure to preach Christ and Him crucified. Once this foundation has been lost then the Church is heading for trouble. The Corinthian leaders were divided and one side had seemingly begun to major on intellectual arguments (wisdom) that affirmed the Christian message. The other side had emphasized signs and wonders.

Such emphases are not wrong in themselves. For example Christians will engage in lively debate with others about creation/evolution, and will also pray fervently for miracles. But in the end it is only through the cross that people will be saved from the power of sin. Christians have things to say about current philosophies and also many amazing stories to tell about angels and healings. Yet the central message that must not be lost is that Christ died for the sins of a lost humanity. The essential foundation of spiritual leadership is the centrality of Christ and Him crucified.

The foolishness of the cross.

To the religious man:

To the religious man the cross is a symbol evoking sympathy. Jesus is portrayed in paintings in His wretched humiliation, but Luke tells us that when Jesus saw women weeping over Him, He implored them not to weep for Him but for themselves and their children (Luke 23:28). Jesus did not die to evoke sympathy, He gave His life in the cosmic battle for the souls of men.

To the philosopher:

To the philosopher there is absolutely no logic in the concept of being cleansed by the blood. God's existence may be deduced from the beauty and order of the created world. Adherence to moral standards also has an arguable logic. But the message of the cross does not rise out of philosophical deduction. It is a startling statement that comes from the whole of scripture as the message of the book, that God did something when Jesus died that has the power to change the eternal destiny of anyone who believes it.

The Centurion's glimpse into glory:

When Christ died Pilate and the Jewish leaders thought that their troublesome enemy had been removed forever from their lives. None of them suspected that something wonderful and history changing had taken place. One of the few to be deeply impressed was the man who had directed the actual procedure of crucifying Jesus: the Roman Centurion. He was unquestionably a hardened man who had seen many die by this cruel method. He was indifferent to Christ and was simply carrying out his orders. Yet Mark and Luke record that the Centurion exclaimed in everyone's hearing : *"Truly this man was the Son of God."* *(Mark 15:39; Matthew 27:54)*. Luke records that the centurion added *"Certainly this was a righteous man!"* *(Luke 23:47)*. The centurion recognized the divinity and holiness of Christ by the manner in which He died. Perhaps others were similarly impressed, and it would be wonderful to know what happened in the mind and soul of Simon of Cyrene as he followed Christ up Calvary's hill bearing His cross (Luke 23:26).

The thief sees through the veil:

Of all present that day the greatest impact was on the man who was crucified beside Him. He recognized that Jesus was a king, an innocent man, and that He was poised on the threshold of a great kingdom over which He had absolute authority. It may be too much to say that He recognized the divinity of Christ, but it is nevertheless true that his last words were in prayer to Jesus. The last words he heard were *"Assuredly, I say to you, today you will be with Me in Paradise." (Luke 23:43)*. The astonishing flash of light that comes through these words is the total assurance of Jesus that He was in control and conscious of where He was going to be in a few hours' time. We may only guess at the impact of those words, but it takes but little imagination to conceive the depth of comfort that came through the forgiveness and total acceptance contained in the words of Jesus. What better way to die than knowing that Jesus is waiting for us in His kingdom?

The absent apostles:

The eleven were scattered. Judas had already died that morning. John alone stood by the cross along with the women. The remaining ten were unaccounted for, probably fearing that they might be arrested and crucified also. The eleven apostles had no understanding of what was taking place. They had never understood Jesus when He had talked of His death. Jesus knew this was the purpose of His being in the world long before these events. His baptism was itself a prophetic act foretelling His death and resurrection. Jesus told His apostles in Matthew 16:21 that He must be killed and rise again. Peter had immediately resisted this as a morbid and negative outcome that must be avoided at all costs (Matthew 16:22). Now that it had happened there was no trace of hope in any of their hearts. They mourned and wept (Mark 16:10) and had no sense that anything good could come from the death of their beloved Master. When Jesus cried out *"It is finished"* His voice had echoed from the highest heaven to the lowest hell declaring that the reign of sin and death was over, that Satan and all his cohorts were overthrown, and that God had righteously opened the door for sinners to be reconciled with God. Angels bowed and worshipped, demons fled in terror, but men remained ignorant of what had just taken place.

For three days the apostles grieved. Then on the third day Jesus rose from the dead. Yet even now they did not perceive this cataclysmic event. The battle had been won on Calvary. His death was the great miracle; it was completely unnatural that the Prince of life should die. He was the Resurrection and the life so how could he die? The Resurrection on the other hand was inevitable, and on this third day Jesus rose, not merely resuscitated to continue life as before, but transformed and bearing in Himself a power that He had obtained in the moments that He hung on the cross. "All authority has been given to Me in heaven and on earth." (Matthew 28:18). Again men did not sense the miracle that had taken place, they had no consciousness of the seismic shift in the courts of eternity. The apostles were not yet ready to preach Christ and Him crucified.

The witnesses:

Not one human being saw what Jesus what was doing when He died. There was no logic to it, it was beyond the reach of the greatest intellects. When He rose again, no one even noticed the event. It had to be announced to the women by the angels, and then by these women to the apostles. It was an unexpected surprise that caught all of His followers off guard. So who are the main witnesses of the cross?

Primary witness 1: Jesus Christ

During His life on earth Jesus spoke of His death as something past:

"God so loved the world that He gave His only begotten Son." John 3:16.

These words were spoken by the Lord at the outset of His ministry between His baptism and His first sermon. Jesus did not say that God loves the world, but that He loved the world. This indicates that something happened before the foundation of the world that is the benchmark for all that God did in creating humanity (Revelation 13:8). Before He created Adam, Jesus had paid the price for every eventuality. This does not mean that Jesus suffered cruel nails and a crown of thorns in heaven. It means that He and the Father secretly agreed this path and that once it was agreed it was as good as done.

What God purposes, is equal to the act itself. Father and Son did not devise the cross after the Fall of Man but before it. Everything that God has ever undertaken in respect to the human race is on the basis of the love of Calvary. So Jesus was a witness of that love that springs from the heart of God. He spoke of Calvary as something already accomplished. This was the mystery kept secret from the foundation of the world. In Romans 16:25 Paul talks of the revelation of *"the mystery kept in silence"* (Revised Version) since the world began. This phrase indicates the hushed awe surrounding the secret of the cross and the glories that would follow it.

When Christ hung on the cross He was made to be sin (2 Corinthians 5:21). Of all who could describe the agony and the victory of the cross, Jesus is the most qualified. Yet in the Resurrection He speaks little of His pain:

"Then He said to them, "Thus it is written, and thus it was necessary for the Christ to suffer and to rise from the dead the third day, and that

repentance and remission of sins should be preached in His name to all nations, beginning at Jerusalem." (Luke 24:46-47)

Jesus was in the calm of a perfect victory.

Primary witness 2: The Father

The Father was the one who made Jesus to be sin (2 Corinthians 5:21). Mercy and grace began in the Father's heart and He planned the salvation of sinners. It was the Father who led Abraham to offer up his son Isaac (Genesis 22) to teach the world His role in offering up His only son Jesus. It was the Father who *"laid on Him the iniquity of us all"* (Isaiah 53:6). The scriptures reveal the cross as is it was experienced by the Father and the Son. What happened there was a covenant between them, that would satisfy their love for righteousness. A conversation in prayer took place on the cross between the Father and the Son. Jesus addressed the Father directly three times:

> *"Father forgive them for they do not know what they do."* (Luke 23:34)
> *"My God, my God why have you forsaken Me?"* (Matthew 27:46)
> *"Father into your hands I commit my spirit."* (Luke 23:46)

These prayers are the basis of our salvation, and we only hear Jesus' side of the conversation. The Father's side can be known through other scriptures:

> *"Yet it pleased the LORD to bruise Him; He has put Him to grief. When You make His soul an offering for sin, He shall see His seed, He shall prolong His days, And the pleasure of the LORD shall prosper in His hand. He shall see the labour of His soul, and be satisfied. By His knowledge My righteous Servant shall justify many, For He shall bear their iniquities."* (Isaiah 53:10-12)

Primary witness 3: The Holy Spirit

The Holy Spirit is the divine recorder of all that happened in the unseen world when Jesus died. He saw into the invisible world of which human beings know so little. The Bible is a carefully crafted witness to the world of the person of God and of His sacrifice to redeem a lost world. Flashes of light come through every part of the book all pointing to this remarkable event. Psalm 22 describes the crucifixion: *"They pierced My hands and My feet,"* (verse 16). It mentions that his clothing was divided but that lots were cast for certain items of clothing (verse 18). The betrayal of Jesus by His brothers was predicted in Genesis (Genesis 37:28). The betrayal by Judas for 30 pieces of silver is described in Psalm 41:9 and Zechariah 11:13. The greatest descriptions of the cross are in Psalm 22 which describes the agony, and Isaiah 53 which describes the purpose of the agony. The Bible describes this event as redemptive. The Messiah is crucified, rejected by His brother Jews, but raised to the highest throne to save the world, including the Gentiles and finally the Jews also. The amazing fact is that all these things were prophesied years before they happened, but were somehow concealed and hidden so that as the events unfolded no one realized what was happening.

The first witnesses from among men

The understanding of the cross in all its implications came on the day of Pentecost when the Holy Spirit was poured out. The apostles became the first human witnesses to the cross. They saw it from the inside, like seeing the back stage of a theatre. The audience see the drama on stage, but those watching from behind understand how everything is done. Apostolic revelation is to see the events of the cross from God's viewpoint.

It was through the baptism with the Holy Spirit that the apostles became witnesses to the death and resurrection of Jesus Christ. This fact has enormous implications. It means that every generation of Christians can have the startling freshness of understanding as if they were eyewitnesses of the events. The truth is that the Holy Spirit gives us more insight into the cross than those who were alive at the time but did not receive the Holy Spirit. One of the great proofs of the veracity of Christianity is the fact that New Testament truth is rediscovered in all its power by different groups which are separated by time and geography. From the Inuit communities of the Arctic to the jungles of Papua New Guinea, from the Hillsong movement in Australia to the Pentecostal Churches of S. America there is a spontaneous re-discovery of the cross and its power to save from the guilt and power of sin.

A further implication is that Christians in all ages have no disadvantage that would hinder them from discovering all the power and freshness of the first Church in the book of Acts. The Bible is the gateway to the discovery of the power of the Spirit that reveals what happened when Christ died two thousand years ago.

The witness of the apostle Paul, and the writer to the Hebrews

Paul and the writer to the Hebrews are the chief witnesses among the apostles to what happened on the cross. God teaches us through these men that it is through the revelation of the Holy Spirit that understanding of these things will come. Paul spent months if not years in Arabia alone with God, and God revealed to him truths that he preached for the rest of his life. Paul received understanding about the Church, about the unity through the gospel of Jew and Gentile in one body and most importantly about the cross.

Six great truths about the cross:

1. **Forgiveness:**
   Christ took the place of every sinner and died as a substitute to obtain forgiveness of sins. (Acts 13:38; 26:18; Ephesians 1:7; Colossians 1:14.)

2. **Cleansing power:**
   Christ broke the power of sin and made it possible for sinners to experience the cleansing power of the blood.
   (1 Corinthians 6:11; Hebrews 9:14)

3. **Union with Christ:**
   Christ identified with sinners so that when He died, they died. Christians can be baptized in to the death of Jesus and die to self, sin and the flesh and lead a Christ centred life.
   (2 Corinthians 5:14-15)

4. **The defeat of death:**
   Christ overcame the power of death itself on the cross to give hope of the resurrection of the dead unto eternal life.
   (Hebrews 2: 9; :2 Timothy 1:10)

5. **The defeat of Satan:**
   Christ overcame powers and principalities on the cross destroying the power of the devil and all his legions.
   (Colossians 2:15; Hebrews 2:9)

6. **Sicknesses are healed by His stripes.**
   This great truth is the foundation of our healing through the sovereign intervention of God. These miracles are an essential part of the Redeeming power of the cross and hence of the gospel. Nevertheless there is an underlying truth that it is only in the coming New Creation that all the effects of sin will be gone forever, and only because of the Blood of Jesus. There will be "no more death, nor sorrow, nor pain for the former things have passed away."
   (Revelation 21:4)

These great truths are all revealed after the coming of the Holy Spirit. The most powerful day in all history was the day Christ died. The most powerful day in human experience is when the power of the cross is revealed to men on their personal day of Pentecost. That day changed the apostles more than anything up to that point. The cross was imprinted on the hearts of the believers by the baptism of the Holy Spirit, and they began to live in the nature of the lamb of God, humbling themselves and loving one another.

Conclusion: Spiritual leadership – ministers of the cross

God needs people who understand by experience and now LIVE this fundamental connection between the cross and the Christian life. Once the cross is removed from the centre carnal behaviour will flourish. There is only one answer and that is the blood of Jesus. It may be that gifted leaders can organize the Church better, along with evangelism and missionary endeavours. But for the work of God the deepest need is for messengers of the cross. Such men will not only preach this message but will have the message impressed upon their hearts. Their conduct will be with Christ like humility. Those who go this way will be quick to repent, to humble themselves and thus be refreshed in the grace of the Lord.

CHAPTER 8

APOSTLES: MINISTERS OF THE HOLY SPIRIT

Peter was given the promise of the keys of the kingdom (Matthew 16:19). This meant that he was to open the door of faith to Israel and then subsequently to Samaria, and then all the nations represented by Cornelius in Acts 10. One of the key elements of opening the door of faith was to introduce the person of the Holy Spirit. Peter had to be taught how to cooperate with God to bring about an outpouring of the Holy Spirit so that a living Church might be formed.

Peter taught by Jesus.

Peter himself was introduced to the Holy Spirit by Jesus Himself. Jesus taught them in the upper room what the Holy Spirit would do when He came. In a long section from chapter 13 – 17 John describes the events of the upper room in the night before Jesus died. It began with Jesus washing their feet and commanding them to love one another. It ended with His great prayer that His followers would have unity with God and each other.

The new community of love: John chapter 13.

The Holy Spirit is not mentioned in chapter 13 when Jesus put on the clothes of a slave and washed the disciples' feet. This was an example to them (John 13:13-14) and they were to humbly love and serve one another as the proof that they were His disciples (John 13:34-35). When the Holy Spirit came on the day of Pentecost the most enduring effect was the creation of a community of selfless love. They shared all things (Acts 2:44-47). They became one in a profound way which has rarely been repeated in history (Acts 4:32-37). The events in the upper room were key lessons on the coming age in which the Holy Spirit would be poured out and a living Church created. This was in marked contrast with the gospels when the apostles argued among themselves and were not in heart unity (Mark 9:33-34). Of all the evidences of a deep work of the Holy Spirit, the greatest is a living assembly where love reigns. All other evidences of the Holy Spirit are meaningless without love (1 Corinthians 13:1-3).

The work of the Holy Spirit (John 14-16).

Jesus expressed to the disciples His longing that they would know the Father and the Son. In John 14:9 Jesus was conscious that they still did not know Him or the Father. This is the great ministry of the Holy Spirit, and Jesus explicitly introduced them to this new dimension of spiritual life in these chapters. There are 8 major aspects to His teaching:

1. **The knowledge of indwelling.**

   "You know Him (the Holy Spirit) for He dwells with you and shall be in you." (John 14:17)

   It is a foundation of evangelical doctrine that those who are saved are indwelt by the Holy Spirit (Romans 8:9). For this reason there is frequently deep distress when believers are taught that it is through the baptism with the Holy Spirit that we know His indwelling. Jesus here tells his believers that they already know the Holy Spirit in a measure. They know Him in their lives, having brought revelation of His person *("You are the Messiah the son of the living God!" Matthew 16:16)*. They know Him in repentance which has worked a deep change of heart leading to salvation (Luke 19:9). Putting these verses alongside Romans 8:9 it is clear that Peter and Zacchaeus along with many others knew the renewing power of the Holy Spirit in their lives. Here Jesus explains this initial experience by saying that the Holy Spirit was with them.

The disciples had an essential foretaste of the Holy Spirit in salvation and then subsequently the fullness in the baptism with the Holy Spirit. If this is properly understood then salvation is a taste of the power of new birth and baptism in the Holy Spirit is the fullness of it. David Pawson in his book "The Normal Christian Birth" argues that there are 4 essential elements to new birth: repentance, faith, baptism in water and baptism with the Holy Spirit. While many agree with David Pawson, it is essential that this understanding should not undermine the believer's assurance of salvation. If this is not understood the whole dimension of leading believers to the fullness of the Spirit is placed on a wrong foundation.

When the thief on the cross died, the words of Jesus were echoing in his ears:

> *"Assuredly, I say to you, today you will be with Me in Paradise."*
> *(Luke 23:43)*

The Holy Spirit had opened his eyes to his sin, to the identity and character of Jesus, and had renewed his heart in salvation. He knew a deep peace with God and assurance of eternal life. He had not yet been baptized with water, and would not have that opportunity. He did not receive the baptism with the Holy Spirit. Some will argue he was an exception. In fact he is demonstrating the rule that salvation is worked between God and man when we bow in repentance and faith and receive Christ as Saviour and Lord.

No Bible interpretation must be allowed to dislodge this essential foundation. It is vital that we have this clear in our minds for the good of our own souls, and to keep alive the skill to lead distressed sinners to salvation.

In this sense the thief on the cross, Zacchaeus and all the disciples had received the Holy Spirit (Romans 8:9). If this understanding be lost then the ministry of the Holy Spirit can easily become a ministry of doubt and fear, rather than joy and assurance. When Philip preached in Samaria the result was great joy (Acts 8:8). When the apostles arrived they did not preach again about repentance, faith and salvation. They simply prayed for the believers to be empowered with the Holy Spirit.

With this in mind it is equally vital not to miss the promise of Jesus that there is a deeper experience of indwelling that we can know through the baptism with the Holy Spirit. Jesus said:

> *"At that day you will know that I am in My Father, and you in Me, and I in you." (John 14:20).*

"That day" is the day when they would experience the baptism with the Holy Spirit. This is perhaps the greatest promise connected with the Holy Spirit and refers to the inner consciousness of the presence of God. The knowledge of God living in us is the key to fruit bearing, since no one can abide in Christ without the conscious awareness of Christ in us. Jesus commanded them to *"Abide in Me and I in you" (John 15:4)*. This command can only be fulfilled if first we are conscious of the indwelling presence of God. This command is the most important key to spiritual growth and fruit bearing. Jesus said that only by this means could we ever bear fruit. This includes the fruit of the Spirit in godly character and influencing other lives to love and follow God.

2. **They will know Him and the Father.**

Jesus assured them that when the Holy Spirit had come Jesus would *"manifest Myself to them." (John 14:21)*. The same verse declares that *"the Father will love them"* indicating that they would experience the love of the Father. Jesus promised them He would not leave them as orphans (John 14:18). Paul said later in Galatians:

> *"And because you are sons, God has sent forth the Spirit of His Son into your hearts, crying out, "Abba, Father!" (Gal 4:6).*

If these verses are interpreted to apply to our lives entirely in salvation it is possible that Christians may miss the deepest and most beautiful dimension of the Holy Spirit. Jesus was opening them up to the ministry of the Holy Spirit that they would receive and which they must pass on. Paul later said that the love of God is poured into our hearts through the Holy Spirit (Romans 5:5). The coming of the Holy Spirit is to bring us into the personal knowledge of the Father's love.

3. **Close relationship in prayer.**

Resulting from this intimate knowledge of God believers can know a deeper place in prayer.

> *"And whatever you ask in My name, that I will do, that the Father may be glorified in the Son. "If you ask anything in My name, I will do it (John 14:13-14).*
> *"And in that day you will ask Me nothing. Most assuredly, I say to*

you, whatever you ask the Father in My name He will give you.
"Until now you have asked nothing in My name. Ask, and you will
receive, that your joy may be full." (John 16:23-24)

The Holy Spirit will make God real, and the result will be that
prayer will be a delight. Of all the promises of the New
Covenant the greatest is the promise of access into the Holy of
Holies (Hebrews 10:19). It would be disastrous if Christians were
to be convinced that they had received the fullness of the Spirit at
conversion only to miss out on the depths of prayer that are open
to us through this deeper work of the Spirit. The need for
intercessors is immeasurably great, and the only one who can take
believers into this realm is the Holy Spirit:

"Likewise the Spirit also helps in our weaknesses. For we do not
know what we should pray for as we ought, but the Spirit Himself
makes intercession for us with groanings which cannot be uttered.
Now He who searches the hearts knows what the mind of the Spirit is,
because He makes intercession for the saints according to the will of
God." (Romans 8:26-27)

4. **Greater works.**

It is a remarkable promise that through the Holy Spirit believers
will do the same works as Jesus and even greater works (John
14:12). Most will be astonished that we can do the same works
let alone greater works. The greater works are surely the things
that follow from the outpouring of the Holy Spirit. Jesus
ministered deliverance from demons, healing, forgiveness of sins
and salvation on such a colossal scale that it would be futile to
imagine that we will do greater miracles of that order. Jesus is
referring to a wholly different order of spiritual power that is
imparted through the baptism with the Holy Spirit. Hearts are
purified, Churches are formed, racial and gender barriers are

dissolved and love reigns in the hearts of God's people. These are the greater works, and they are achieved through the deeper union with God and the resulting power in prayer that is the inheritance of God's people.

5. **The Holy Spirit teaches and guides.**

This promise is repeated by John in his first letter:

> *"But the anointing which you have received from Him abides in you, and you do not need that anyone teach you; but as the same anointing teaches you concerning all things, and is true, and is not a lie, and just as it has taught you, you will abide in Him." (1 John 2:27)*

The most remarkable thing about John's statement is the apparent contradiction. He "teaches" them through his letter that they don't need anyone to teach them. Equally there is a spiritual gift of teaching (Ephesians 4:11; 1 Corinthians 12:28) and Paul taught the Church in Antioch for a whole year (Acts 11:26). The solution to this paradox lies in the fact that there are things that the Holy Spirit cannot teach, and things that only He can teach. He does not teach us the contents of the Bible, nor the Hebrew and Greek languages in which it is written. But He does teach the knowledge of God and He does make God real to us, and no teacher can do this. These two dimensions of teaching are to overlap in the teaching and preaching ministry in the Church. Individuals are to teach the Bible while at the same time praying and trusting that there will be a dimension to their words which only God can deliver.

The Holy Spirit teaches and guides the believers through many different means, but the chief means is through the "witness of the Spirit" or the inner "anointing" by which we "know" things. John writes that by this inner anointing we "know all things". He does not mean we know Church History or that we no longer need to hear preaching and teaching! John is referring to things that not only are known by the inner anointing, they can only be known by this means. By the inner witness we know we are children of God (Romans 8:16). By this inner witness believers can sense a deceiving spirit (1 John 2:18-20.) Of course we use our minds to detect wrong doctrines, but we know wrong spirits by the anointing. Not everyone who has a strange doctrine is of a wrong spirit, and not everyone who has right doctrine has a right spirit!

The inner witness frequently leads believers to make choices in their lives. Acts 16:6-7 describes the apostles as they seek to discern the next place for them to preach the gospel. The Holy Spirit communicates His will to them, perhaps through the inner faculty of knowing or perhaps through some other means. Occasionally a believer will experience supernatural guidance through a dream, a vision or an audible voice. But the believer judges whether these phenomena are from God by the inner witness. The witness of the Spirit is greater than a voice or a prophecy.

6. **"The Helper... will testify, you will testify" John 15:26-27. "He will glorify Me." John 16:14.**

> *"But when the Helper comes, whom I shall send to you from the Father, the Spirit of truth who proceeds from the Father, He will testify of Me. And you also will bear witness, because you have been with Me from the beginning." (John 15:26-27)*

By this Jesus indicates the principal work of the Holy Spirit which is to testify of Jesus. When Jesus is exalted the Holy Spirit is at work. He loves Jesus deeply and works to make Him known to all mankind. The Holy Spirit takes the things of Jesus matchless personality and imparts them to wondering disciples. These are the pearls that are not thrown before swine. When Christians bear testimony it is through the inward awareness of Jesus. Just as the early apostles were eye witnesses of Jesus' resurrection, so through the Holy Spirit, all believers are witnesses of the person of Christ as a living reality in their lives.

7. **He will convict the world of sin, righteousness and judgment.**

> *"And when He has come, He will convict the world of sin, and of righteousness, and of judgment: of sin, because they do not believe in Me; of righteousness, because I go to My Father and you see Me no more; of judgment, because the ruler of this world is judged." (John 16:8-11)*

Conviction of sin is an essential component of leading people to salvation. It is the awareness of how much we have offended God combined with the hope that God is able to change us.

> *Smith Wigglesworth on a train:*
>
> *"I was travelling to Cardiff in South Wales. I had been much in prayer on the journey. The carriage was full of people whom I knew to be unsaved, but as there was so much talking and joking I could not get in a word for my Master. As the train was nearing the station, I thought I would wash my hands... and as I returned to the carriage, a man jumped up and said, 'Sir, you convince me of sin,' and fell on his knees there and then. Soon the whole carriage of people were crying out the same way. They said, 'Who are you? What are you? You convince us all of sin'..." (Stanley Frodsham, "Smith Wigglesworth, Apostle of Faith" page 80).*

A moral person will show to others merely what is right and wrong while a person full of the Holy Spirit presents a different order of life. The one who believes in Jesus has an inward purity of heart and a devotion to Christ. The process of conviction of sin is through the beautiful presence of Christ in the believer.

Charles Finney at a factory in Utica.

"*I went to the factory to walk through it. As I went through, I observed a great deal of agitation among those who were busy at their work. On passing through an area where a large number of young women were weaving, I observed one women eyeing me, then making a comment to her neighbour. They both laughed. I could see that they were quite agitated by my presence. I went slowly toward them, with sorrow filling my eyes. As the one woman saw me coming, her hands trembled so that she could not do her work. I approached slowly, looking and acting like I was interested in the machinery on each side. This girl grew more and more agitated...trying to calm herself, she looked out the window. When I came within eight or ten feet of her, I looked solemnly at her. She sank down to her knees and burst into tears. The impression caught almost like gunpowder, and in a few moments nearly everyone in the room was in tears. The feeling spread throughout the factory. The owner of the factory said, 'stop the mill, and let the people be attended to...it is more important that our souls be saved than that the factory run.'*"

8. The Great Condition for receiving the Spirit – loving Jesus.

"If you love Me, keep My commandments. And I will pray the Father, and He will give you another Helper, that He may abide with you forever, the Spirit of truth, whom the world cannot receive, because it neither sees Him nor knows Him; but you know Him, for He dwells with you and will be in you." (John 14:15-17)

The New Testament gives instruction on how to receive the Holy Spirit. We must repent (Acts 2:38), obey (Acts 5:31), thirst (John 7:37), believe (John 7:38), and finally ask! (Luke 11:13). This summary of how to receive the Holy Spirit is biblical and accurate. But it is only technical. Imagine someone asking: "How does a person get married?" The answer is: register the intended wedding, go to a Church, go through the vows etc.... But all these things miss the point. The first requirement is to meet someone and fall in love! In the same way the Holy Spirit is given to those who love Jesus. Jesus said that if we love Him He will take care of the rest. Love is to make our supreme choice of one thing over all others. Love is a powerful tug in the heart that makes people think constantly of the one they love. Love is a heart melted and drawn under the influence of the person they love. People in love will do amazing and unusual things to win the love of someone. Christ died through love, and His followers respond to that amazing love and are filled with the Holy Spirit as they yield to the love that burgeons in their hearts.

Peter waiting for the coming of the Holy Spirit.

In the forty days of His resurrection appearances Jesus prophesied the imminent outpouring of the Spirit. He commanded the apostles to wait in Jerusalem, and assured them that only a few days would pass before they would be baptised with the Holy Spirit (Acts 1:5). In preparation for this He breathed on them and told them to receive the Holy Spirit (John 20:22). They did not receive the baptism in the Holy Spirit at that moment and there is no reference by the apostles to that moment in the Acts or the epistles. They may have received a refreshing of their faith at that moment, or it may be that Jesus was indicating to them that when the Holy Spirit came they were to receive Him as easily as breathing. By this prophetic act Jesus possibly reminded them of the moment when Adam received the breath of life from the mouth of God (Genesis 2:7). (The word "spirit" in Hebrew (ruach) and in Greek (pneuma) can be translated as breath).

Peter waited for 10 days with the eleven, but he never subsequently taught that it was necessary to "tarry" or wait for the Holy Spirit. The coming of the Holy Spirit was promised to all who repent (Acts 2:38). It may be that some believers will find that they must seek God for some time in order to receive the Holy Spirit. However this is not a condition of receiving the Holy Spirit, it is simply a process that some must go through to position their hearts to receive in faith. Such a process may involve deep heart searching regarding sins and attitudes that must be repented of in order to receive.

Peter received the Holy Spirit.

Peter received the Holy Spirit on the day of Pentecost. He spoke with tongues in a supernatural manner which was evidenced by the fact that people from different language groups heard them speak in their own tongue (Acts 2:4 & 8). It is therefore remarkable that Jesus and the apostles nowhere taught that speaking in tongues was the primary evidence of the coming of the Holy Spirit. Many believers and Bible teachers believe that speaking in tongues is the essential sign. This is built on the assumption that Peter and the apostles thought it to be self-evident and did not need to be expressed. Others believe that the main sign of the baptism with the Holy Spirit is love (1 Corinthians 13:1). Surely the best means of uniting these two positions is to accept each other's view with humility and tolerance, and most importantly allow a diversity of views among believers. In fact the gift that is mentioned with most emphasis is prophecy. Peter quoted Joel's prophecy extensively in which God said:

> *"I will pour out My Spirit in those days; and they shall prophesy."*
> *(Acts 2:18)*

At the very least speaking in tongues should be given the same prominence as Jesus and the apostles gave it when they spoke about the Holy Spirit. It is an important gift, but there are other evidences of the Holy Spirit. The worst disaster for any movement would be to have extensive use of the gifts but little proof of spiritual character in holiness, love and self-denial. This was the tragedy of Corinth. A careful study of Corinthians indicates that the Church had abandoned the spiritual foundation of Christ and Him crucified. The result was carnal behaviour and among many other things, misuse of the gifts.

In Acts 15 Peter recounted the outpouring of the Holy Spirit in the house of Cornelius. (They too had spoken with tongues in Acts 10:46, though there is no evidence that any known language was recognised on that occasion). He compares the event with his own experience on the day of Pentecost using phrases such as *"giving them the Holy Spirit, just as He did to us." (Acts 15:8).* The remarkable observation Peter made is that *"God made no distinction between us and them, purifying their hearts by faith." (Acts 15:9).* This is significant because it was not an outward sign, and yet it is Peter's clearest affirmation of what happened to him on the day of Pentecost. His memory of that day was that God had purified his heart. This is what God had promised in Ezekiel 36:25-27.

****

Les Wheeldon – my baptism with the Holy Spirit.

I gave my life to Jesus Christ in a step of personal surrender in May 1973. I was in my last year of High School and had become friends with a student named Malcolm Love. His father was Pastor Brian Love who served as a Baptist minister in the nearby village of Measham. Malcolm had witnessed to me about Jesus, and had started a small Christian group in the college. He played recordings of Billy Graham, and shared the message of the gospel and whether he knew it or not, his words found a home in my heart. So it was that alone in my room I gave my life to Christ. I realised immediately that God had changed something deep in my heart. I now had a thirst to know the Bible and the direction of my life was towards God. I attended the Baptist Church and was baptised a year later in September 1974. But I was aware of a hardness of heart and a deep spiritual need.

In October 1974 I went to Oxford University and there I met some spirit-filled believers including a man named Andrew Simpkins who was the leader of the Christian Union. His life radiated a love for Jesus and His word that disarmed me and awakened a thirst for more spiritual reality in my own life. Andrew was very sensitive and waited several months before gently challenging me to seek God for the baptism with the Holy Spirit.

I spent one long night in prayer asking God to fill me with His Holy Spirit. I was deeply touched that night, and some friends encouraged me to launch out in tongues. I did begin to speak with tongues by faith, but deep in my heart I was not satisfied. There had to be more. I felt a need for power to live, not just gifts of the Spirit.

So I kept seeking and it was on 14 May 1975 in my room at Oxford that I received a powerful baptism with the Holy Spirit. Waves of love and power swept over me, and it felt as if they were welling up from deep within my own heart as well as pouring out from above. I was overwhelmed with a sense of being washed in my heart. I was also conscious of the presence of Jesus. The Holy Spirit was cleansing me and focusing me on the wonderful person of Jesus Christ whose presence was so overwhelmingly real to me. The result was that I worshipped Him and poured out my heart. I was so overcome with the awareness of Him that I could not sleep that night but worshipped on and on.

The ongoing effect of this experience was to make prayer the sweetest joy of my life and I spent hours in His presence being quietened and changed as I waited on God and His word. I realise that it is not God's will to exalt our experiences as these will vary from person to person. Nevertheless, though some will have less sense of a sudden change than others, it is vital that we know God and His presence by experience. Jesus said that we would know the coming of the Holy Spirit, and this can only mean "know by experience." We know many things by books, but we must know the baptism with the Holy Spirit by experience.

****

Peter in Samaria and Caesarea.

Peter along with John led the believers in Samaria to receive the Holy Spirit (Acts 8:14-17). He then also "led" Cornelius to receive the Holy Spirit in Acts 10:44. Very little detail is recounted of what was said in Samaria. Peter's word to Cornelius in Acts 10 is a concise summary of the main facts about Jesus Christ: His Lordship (Acts 10:36), His power (Acts 10:38), His death and Resurrection (Acts 10:39-41) and His role as Judge of the whole human race (Acts 10:42). Peter's final word is that through Christ comes forgiveness of sins (Acts 10:43), and it is at that moment that the Holy Spirit was poured out on Cornelius and the assembled household. The events in Samaria and in Caesarea were dramatic and visible to all. Something very powerful happened. In Samaria salvation and Spirit baptism were two separate events. In Caesarea they happened simultaneously.

Why then was the apostolic input so significant? After all, Paul received the Holy Spirit without any apostle present (Acts 9:17). Moreover it is surely not wrong to assume that the Ethiopian Eunuch received the Holy Spirit through Philip's ministry in Acts 9:35-39. It hardly seems possible that God would allow this first African believer to continue his journey alone without the fullness of the Holy Spirit. The fact is that such powerful events as the outpourings in Samaria and Caesarea needed skilful and wise oversight. Before we think of Peter as a wise old sage, it must be remembered that Peter was himself learning through these events. He was often taught by the words that came out of his mouth spontaneously. (Peter did not deliver his sermon in Acts 2 from a carefully crafted speech he had prepared the night before Pentecost!) In Caesarea he was himself astonished that the Holy Spirit was poured out on Gentiles and had to think on his feet to acknowledge the new thing that God was doing (Acts 10:44-48).

In subsequent outpourings in history, human beings have often been overwhelmed by the power of the Holy Spirit. Not all such events have had the competent oversight of ministers who can discern between the true power of God and the exuberant and occasionally carnal human reaction to it. This is especially true when outpourings occur on large gatherings. People have fallen down, filled with ecstasy, speaking uncontrollably in tongues. Such events have been documented during the Wesleyan Revival, the Azusa Street outpouring, the Welsh and Hebridean Revival along with more recent phenomena such as the "Toronto blessing." It is at times like these that leaders who are skilful and experienced in the ministry of the Spirit are needed. There can be few movements where the Holy Spirit moves in power that will not face challenging moments. At such times leaders must lead in such a manner that supernatural phenomena are not discouraged, while steering believers away from confusion and chaotic behaviour onto the solid ground of scripture.

Peter's gift and calling: a minister of the Spirit.

Peter was a man in whom God had dug deep and opened up powerful wells of the Holy Spirit. This is what Jesus referred to on the last day of the feast of Tabernacles:

> *"On the last day, that great day of the feast, Jesus stood and cried out, saying, "If anyone thirsts, let him come to Me and drink. He who believes in Me, as the Scripture has said, out of his heart will flow rivers of living water." (John 7:37-38)*

There are many believers who drink of the wells that flow from others, and this is not wrong, but each local Church must have this ministry of the Spirit flowing in their lives and in their meetings. If this is absent the Church will stagnate. Peter somehow had grasped the keys to obtaining an outpouring and maintaining it. Most important of all, Peter had no trust in His own virtue or spiritual qualities. In his sermon in Acts 2 Peter preached Christ and Him crucified as the finished work that was sufficient to enable repentant people to be forgiven and filled with the Holy Spirit. There was no strain in Peter, he was at rest in the floods of grace that had been poured out on him.

Paul and the ministry of the Spirit.

Paul demonstrates this apostolic gift and wisdom in his letters to the Corinthians. Paul speaks in 2 Corinthians 3 of the ministry of the Spirit as being a central characteristic of the whole ministry of the New Covenant. There are 4 aspects to this ministry which he outlines in this chapter:

1. **The source of this ministry.** Paul contrasts the ministry of the Spirit with the ministry of the Law through Moses. The ministry of the Law is of the letter, and as such it cannot give life (2

Corinthians 3:6). The minister of the Spirit has entered within the veil into the conscious realm of the Holy Spirit. He himself beholds the Lord with an unveiled face and is being transformed from glory to glory (2 Corinthians 3:18). The minister of dry Christianity looks at books, while the minister of life looks at Christ through a heart that has passed into another dimension of life with God. At its most basic level the minister of the Spirit is a man or woman of prayer. Dry Christianity is not necessarily boring and dull. It may be enlivened by humour, anecdotes or theatrical pathos. There are many speakers who have the ability to move their audience with great oratorical skill, but lack the ability to bring revelation from the presence of God.

2. **The power of this ministry.** Paul again contrasts the effect of the ministry with the Law of Moses.

> *"You are our epistle written in our hearts, known and read by all men; clearly you are an epistle of Christ, ministered by us, written not with ink but by the Spirit of the living God, not on tablets of stone but on tablets of flesh, that is, of the heart." 2 Corinthians 3:2-3.*

Here Paul reminds the readers of the power of God's finger to write on stone as if it were butter. God's power can inscribe the hardest substance, and the hardest substance is the human heart. Words spoken in the power of the Holy Spirit change the character and the nature of the hearers. God writes on the hearts of all who wait on Him, and such are changed simply by tarrying in His presence. Ministers of the Spirit speak words that change lives and make them to be living letters that declare the person of Christ. True ministry of the Spirit reaches the heart.

3. **Utter dependence on the Holy Spirit.** Paul explains that no one can become self-sufficient or expert in this ministry. Techniques will always fall short, and the only way to minister life

is to be in total dependence on God. This means that weakness is an advantage, and our strengths can easily hinder the flow of power that is so needed:

> *"Not that we are sufficient of ourselves to think of anything as being from ourselves, but our sufficiency is from God, who also made us sufficient as ministers of the new covenant, not of the letter but of the Spirit; for the letter kills, but the Spirit gives life." (2 Corinthians 3:5-6).*

4. The Glory of God is manifest.

> *"But if the ministry of death, written and engraved on stones, was glorious, so that the children of Israel could not look steadily at the face of Moses because of the glory of his countenance, which glory was passing away, how will the ministry of the Spirit not be more glorious? For if the ministry of condemnation had glory, the ministry of righteousness exceeds much more in glory. For even what was made glorious had no glory in this respect, because of the glory that excels." (2 Corinthians 3:7-10)*

Paul says that in this ministry there is a far greater glory than anything Moses knew. This is a great claim, and reminds us of the prayer of Moses that he might see God's glory (Exodus 33:18). After Moses had seen the glory of God his face shone such that he veiled his face while talking with his fellow Israelites. Paul says that the ministry of the Spirit is the impartation of a greater glory. When a person is moved to speak from the direct presence of God in their hearts, the listeners are carried into another realm in which glory touches them. Glory is that which is overwhelming, sweeping aside unbelief and swallowing it up in the tide of God's presence. When the Holy Spirit is ministered congregations sometimes sit in awed silence at the majesty of

God. At other times there will be strong conviction of sin, with people falling on their knees, or on their faces before God.

Conclusion

The understanding of the ministry of the Holy Spirit is an essential foundation of the New Testament Church. If ministers lack understanding then there will be a rapid drift away from the power of the Spirit, and descent into either mere intellectualism or into a superficial obsession with the manifestations of the Holy Spirit. How vital it is that believers receive the overwhelming power of the Spirit with all the amazing manifestations of gifts and joy. How vital too that leaders be able to lead their congregations to obtain outpourings of the Holy Spirit.

At the same time it is vital that believers be steered to look not at the gifts but at the giver, that they treat the manifestations as passing phenomena that are as nothing compared with knowing Christ. Ministers of the Spirit are aware that human beings may react immaturely when the Holy Spirit is poured out and will seek to point believers to the Lord and anchor them securely in His word. When Mary Magdalene sought Jesus on Resurrection morning she was not impressed with the angels; she had her sights set on something far greater. She said to Jesus whom she presumed to be the gardener:

"Tell me where you have laid Him and I will take Him away." (John 20:15)

As believers look with unswerving faith at Jesus and His cross the Holy Spirit will be poured out.

PART III

~

PRACTICAL CONSIDERATIONS

"Labour to gather a Church alive for Jesus, every member energetic to the full, and the whole in incessant activity for the salvation of men. To this end there must be the best of preaching to feed the host into strength, continual prayer to bring down the power from on high, and the most heroic example on your own part to fire their zeal: then, under the divine blessing, a common-sense management of the entire force cannot fail to produce the most desirable issues. Who among you can grasp this idea and embody it in actual fact?"

C.H. Spurgeon.

CHAPTER 9 – THE ART OF LEADERSHIP: MANAGING CHANGE

> *"If you haven't changed your mind recently, have you ever stopped to ask if you have one?"* (Seen on a car bumper sticker)

Churches are not exempt from the conflicts and struggles that afflict human society. As each generation passes, society changes; but it may be true to say that the 21st century has brought with it the greatest changes ever seen - because of the internet, social media and networking. In all ages differences in style of dress and music have been battle grounds between generations of different taste. The great question is how is the Church to handle change? If this question is not faced then leaders may well find that they are either dividing the Church unnecessarily or compromising the heart of the gospel.

Change was flooding through the Church in the first century. This was because the age of law (the Old Testament or Covenant) was giving way to the era of grace (the New Testament or Covenant). If ever a generation came under strain then it was the first century, and in some measure this strain has continued even to the present day. For those who followed Christ the pace was exciting and probably at times scary. Christ was not afraid to challenge the taboos of the culture of His day. When He spoke with the woman of Samaria He exposed the chauvinism of the disciples who were astounded that He spoke with a woman (John 4:27). The woman herself was taken aback that He a Jewish man was talking with her a Samaritan woman (John 4:9). On another occasion Jesus demonstrated that He had no interest in maintaining the Pharisees' laws of hand washing that were more to do with flaunting their supposed spirituality than hygiene (Mark 7:2-3). He constantly challenged the attitudes of all those around him by His example: He touched a leper (Matthew 8:3), a bleeding woman (Mark 5:27), and a dead body (Mark 5:41; Luke 7:14).

What kinds of issues challenge the Church of the twenty first century? Many Churches are in disagreement about the musical element of Church worship. Some detest drums while others cannot imagine good worship without them. Some Churches have experienced frequent battles of the song books, and staying up to date is a major challenge. There are always changes going on in the whole realm of fashion. In some Churches a suit and tie are absolute requirements for preaching while in others torn jeans are the accepted uniform! Then there are disputes about which is the best Bible translation. The King James Version still has fervent supporters who are convinced that the other translations are so corrupted that they are unusable. Then there are the weightier issues of sexual morality. Homosexuality is the most contentious of issues, but it is not the only realm of controversy. There are disputes about divorce, ordination of women, etc...

So why is leadership the management of change? The answer is that change is here to stay and leaders must lead their Churches into relevance and contemporary expressions of the wonderful message of the gospel. But equally there are things about the Christian message that will never change. Once they have been tampered with, the gospel is lost and the Church is irrelevant whether or not she is popular and contemporary.

Eight Key principles of change management.

Principle 1: When two worlds collide - understanding the battle ground.

The 21st century is in the grip of the greatest period of change that has ever been seen in the history of the world. The underlying philosophy of this age may be labelled "post-modern existentialism." Yet if 90% of ordinary people were asked to define this philosophy they would not know where to begin. (In fact few philosophers agree on a definition!) In short this is the philosophy of the individual shaping his philosophical and moral values around their personal thoughts, feelings and experiences. It can best be understood by the way it has re-shaped our modern life style.

What are the main elements of the world view of the 21st century?

- Opinion is King. By our own will and choice we create our own universe, our own heaven and hell. Life is what you make of it.

- There are no absolutes: no moral right and wrong and no one has the right to preach, to authoritatively declare, to teach and inform. Sexual morality is blurred. Fornication is not a sin. Common behaviour is a guide to forming opinions.

- The basis of truth is now through consensus and discussion. No one has the truth! If it feels right - do it.

- Self-realisation, a world view that puts me at the centre.

- Consumerism is decisive. "I buy therefore I am." I have consumer rights if I "buy into" a Church program. I shop around for the right Church. I have consumer rights and expect a good return, or I will go where there are better bargains to be had.

This world view promotes diversity as a virtue. It is crucial that leaders understand the pressure that is on the Church to allow change for its own sake to become the heart and centre of everything. This would be to allow worldliness not only to influence the Church but to take it over.

This world view is in direct conflict with the Christian world view which has the following elements:

- Our opinion is irrelevant, God is King and His will is to be honoured and obeyed above all else.

- The world is built on absolutes that cannot be changed but are the will of the Creator and designer of the human race.

- Truth comes through revelation and the main source of truth is the Bible.

- Worshipping God, exalting Christ, finding out what pleases Him are the heart and centre of life.

- I give myself in surrender to the Saviour who died for me.

The Christian Church comes under subtle pressure to mix these two world views.

Take the following question as an example:

Why do believers go to Church?
- To get good experience?
- Comforting preaching?
- Convenient times?
- Get blessed, built up?
- Social network?
- Employment?

In fact there is only one answer: we go to meetings for God not for me:

- For His glory.
- To worship Him.
- To bless others.
- To serve and not be served.
- To satisfy His heart.

In understanding the way in which these two worlds collide leaders will be better placed to challenge the believers to lay aside values which are not Christian. At the same time understanding the conflict will equip leaders to relate to the world around.

The "Y" generation – a new mission field.

To add to the pressures on the modern leader there are a whole array of phrases which are hard to master. The "Y" generation is the phrase referring to people born in the 80s and early 90s. (They are the "Y" generation because they follow the "X" generation which was born in the 60s and 70s). The "Y" generation are also known as the internet generation. They are at home with social media and communicate/network extensively by the internet on mobile phones etc.

Various studies show that this generation is less likely to have been to a Church service. This is a generation that has few philosophical absolutes to undergird life. The world of social media offers immediate sharing of experience, but few philosophical or spiritual sign posts to fill an inner vacuum. At the same time there is in society a growing moral chaos with alcohol and drugs readily available and little or no teaching on how to develop strong relationships in marriage as a safe environment for sexual fulfilment. One result is a rise in mental problems such as self-harming and depression.

In reaching out to this generation it is easy to become discouraged and even bury one's head in one's hands or worst of all the sand. The answer is to realise that Christians still have exactly what every age group is ultimately looking for.

> *"Within this often spiritually bleak and challenging landscape another ray of light appears. Generation Y people, like all human beings, need relationships and specifically trusted relationships. Generation Y may not trust Church but Christians who come across as authentic, who live out a different sense of values, and talk of a God found in personal experience, are people they may find interesting, able to trust, and be willing to talk to."*
> *Andrew Simpkins: The Y Generation: A Dummies Guide for Aging Pastors, Journal of Missional Practice.*

While the Church may not embrace the world view of the 21st century, it is vital that we understand it in order to be able to reach out to what is "an unreached people group" that has grown up on our doorstep. Just as a missionary to some remote tribe will seek to understand the people he is trying to influence, so too leaders must realise that while the gospel remains the same, their approach must change. Paul quoted from the Greek poets and philosophers when speaking to the crowds in Athens. In the same way leaders must understand and reach out to the new mission field that has grown up around us.

Principle 2: Rediscovering the moral compass.

The Bible is the foundation and source of truth and can be relied upon for accurate information. The 20th/21st century has suffered a catastrophic loss of direction - there is no compass. Some Christians have become open to new ideas which are held to be of equal value to the Bible, e.g. words from angels, dreams and visions. Many

Christians no longer ask, *"Is it in the Bible?"* As in Jeremiah's day, there is a tragic rise in false prophecies. Prophets are prophesying from their own imagination, not from the Lord. Prophets prophesy peace when there is no peace and *'heal the hurt of the people slightly'* *(Jeremiah 6:14)*

The whole question of handling change in the Church can only be faced if there is a radical turning to the foundation of the scriptures as the only source of truth in a confused world.

Why is the Bible so important?

Smith Wigglesworth said: *"God's Word is supernatural in origin, eternal in duration, inexpressible in valour, infinite in scope, regenerative in power, infallible in authority, universal in application, inspired in totality. Read it through; write it down; pray it in; work it out; pass it on. The Word of God changes a man until he becomes an epistle of God."*

John Wesley said: *"I want to know one thing – the way to heaven; how to land safely on that happy shore. God Himself has condescended to teach the way; for this very end He came from heaven. He has written it down in a book. O give me that Book! At any price give me the Book of God!"*

The Bible is Inspired by the Holy Spirit:
(2 Timothy 3:16; 2 Peter 1:20-21)

Many have opposed the Bible by asserting that it is the work of human beings. However, there are 24,000 manuscripts which confirm that the Bible has come down through the generations with no changes. Among ancient documents there is none that comes anywhere near the massive weight of evidence for the accuracy of the Bible. Homer's Iliad is the nearest rival, and for that there are only 643 manuscripts, with major differences.

Here are a few quotes on the authority of the Bible:

Thomas Arnold (English Historian):

145

"I know of no one fact in the history of mankind which is proved by better and fuller evidence than the Resurrection of Jesus Christ."

Sir Frederick Kenyon, Director of the British Museum:
"The last foundation for any doubt that the Scriptures have come down to us as they were written now has been removed. Both the authenticity and the general integrity of the New Testament may now be regarded as firmly established."

Dr Simon Greenleaf of Harvard University tried to refute the New Testament and the accounts of Jesus Christ. He became utterly convinced that they were true and accurate documents, and said:
"The Resurrection of Jesus Christ is one of the best established events of history according to the laws of legal evidence administered in the courts of justice."

The revival in Josiah's day was preceded by the rediscovery of the word of God (2 Chronicles 34:15). The reformation in Europe was provoked by a massive distribution of the scriptures in the language of the common people. Wherever the Bible was made accessible there was a widespread move of the Holy Spirit.

Principle 3: Distinguishing the eternal - from the temporary

Human beings have a terrible capacity to major on the minor! Churches sometimes defend their temporary culture more than the truths contained in the Bible.

In medical universities students are sometimes invited to observe top surgeons performing operations. Once, the students were enthralled by the skill of the visiting professor as he talked them through the procedure pausing to point out various details as he cut into the abdomen of the patient. As he finished the operation there was a rapturous round of applause from the assembled students. Quietly the anaesthetist whispered in the ear of the surgeon "he's dead." The lesson is simple: we can get so obsessed with our methods that we forget the most important thing – our relationship with God and other people.

Distinguishing the eternal from the temporary is not always easy, but there are some areas that obviously cannot be changed.

- God is the Creator, and humanity is a special creation.
- Man is a fallen creature, a sinner needing a saviour.
- Christ is God's son and God in human form.
- Christ died on the cross for the sins of the whole world.
- Those who repent and believe in Him are justified and accepted by God.
- God sent the Holy Spirit to apply the cleansing power of the blood of Jesus in the hearts of those who believe.
- Christ will return again to this world at the end of time.
- Christ will judge the human race at the end of time, and the human race will be divided between heaven and hell.

The list is much longer and these truths are just a sample of things that cannot be changed. Paul the apostle was totally uncompromising when it came to the gospel of salvation. He was willing to oppose Peter publicly risking a split on the question of salvation by works or by faith (Galatians 2:14-16). He would have divided the Church on this issue and sadly this has been necessary in history. The most notable example is the Reformation. When Luther said "Here I stand I can do no other" he was referring to his discovery of truths that had been lost in the Roman Catholic Church of the middle ages. Luther was willing to die rather than deny these biblical foundations.

The things which are passing away are the elements of culture that grow up around the practices and traditions of the Church. Our dress code for meetings, our preference in various musical styles and instruments are easy to identify. It is astonishing how fiercely some Christians will cling to outward forms as foundations of their faith in Christ. It is precisely in these areas that one must learn the art of compromise.

Principle 4: The art of compromise

Paul was a lion for the truth but he also said one thing that is the very essence of compromise:

"I have become all things to all men" (I Corinthians 9:22)

Paul realized the value of a soul. He compromised on so many areas in order to win souls to Christ.

"For though I am free from all men, I have made myself a servant to all, that I might win the more; And to the Jews I became as a Jew, that I might win Jews; to those who are under the law, as under the law, that I might win those who are under the law; to those who are without law, as without law (not being without law toward God, but under law toward Christ), that I might win those who are without law; to the weak I became as weak, that I might win the weak. I have become all things to all men, that I might by all means save some."
(1 Corinthians 9:19-22)

Paul was speaking as an evangelist when he wrote these words. This was clearly his master passion: to win souls to Christ. He was adaptable and ready to change anything that was secondary in order to fulfil his mission.

"If the gospel is to be understood....if it is to be received as something which communicates the truth about the real human situation, if it is as we say "to make sense," it has to be communicated in the language of those to whom it is addressed and it has to be clothed in symbols which are meaningful to them."
Lesslie Newbigin, The Gospel in a Pluralist Society, (London: SPCK, 1989)

Principle 5: Eating pork

Peter was the first leader in the New Testament to realize that the gospel must not be packaged in laws that disguise or even blur the gospel of grace. Peter himself was reluctant to take this road. In Acts 10 God showed him a vision of a sheet coming down from heaven containing various kinds of unclean food. Whether there was pork, prawns, snakes, camels or dogs in the sheet is not clear. What is clear is Peter's horror at the thought of eating the food that he saw. Moreover Peter objected that he had never eaten such food in his life. This was the one commandment that he could boast about and now God was telling him to break these Old Testament dietary laws. What was at stake was the future of the Church. If Peter could not break out of his prejudices then the Church would remain a small Jewish sect and have no impact on the Gentiles. In the same way, if leaders and congregations are not willing to sacrifice their prejudices, the Church will become narrow and relevant only to a decreasing number of people.

At this point it is vital to remember that this readiness to change cuts both ways. Willingness to change means that we can eat things that were once forbidden, and also give up things that are normally allowed. For example, Peter and Paul would never have eaten pork with a Jewish family out of a desire to win them to Christ. But they were willing to eat anything if it opened anyone's heart to believe. Older believers must identify with youth culture to win them to Christ. Young believers must equally identify with older generations to lead them into the blessings of the gospel. This willingness to compromise must lead to a joyous abandon of secondary issues in order that Christ be glorified.

God wants the Church to flourish as a Church for all nations and all generations. God wants a Church where Jew and Gentile are one. God wants a Church of Abraham, Isaac and Jacob, three generations serving the living God together. To attain this, the Church must return to the altar that stands at the centre of all in God's kingdom. On that altar we must offer ourselves, our prejudices, our culture including our likes and dislikes. The price is small compared with the sacrifice of Christ, when He laid aside His glory to identify with a fallen humanity in the incarnation. He offered His perfect humanity to God as a sacrifice to change the hearts of human beings.

It is easy to write about general ideas, but often it is a difficult choice of whom we offend, not if we offend. We may offend people in the Church by identifying with unsaved people. Or we turn off unsaved people by yielding to the legalistic demands of sections of the Church. Sadly on occasions it is impossible to bring every believer to find the delight of what God is doing right before our eyes. We have to admit that we are all slow learners:

> ""*We played the flute for you, and you did not dance; we mourned to you, And you did not lament." For John came neither eating nor drinking, and they say, "He has a demon." The Son of Man came eating and drinking, and they say, "Look, a glutton and a winebibber, a friend of tax collectors and sinners!""* (Matthew 11:17-19)

Principle 6: Facing absolutes: Human sexuality

Sexuality is potentially the most powerful force in a human soul. Once this genie is out of the bottle it is hard to tame. The human race has broken the Creator's guidelines on sexuality in every generation, and there is little evidence to suggest that one generation is essentially worse than another. Many have idealistic ideas about the Victorian era, but a study of the morals of that period quickly reveals that the Victorians were masters at living double lives. Christianity was a veneer, and under the surface passions bubbled away.

God's guidelines for sexuality are immutable. If there is compromise in this area then the foundation of salvation itself will be lost. It would be a disaster if leaders taught that biblical standards of sexual morality were of secondary importance. Paul describes God's unchanging standards when he says:

> *"Do you not know that the unrighteous will not inherit the kingdom of God? Do not be deceived. Neither fornicators, nor idolaters, nor adulterers, nor homosexuals, nor sodomites, nor thieves, nor covetous, nor drunkards, nor revilers, nor extortioners will inherit the kingdom of God." 1 Corinthians 6:9-10.*

This and other passages affirm that there are standards of sexual morality that are unchanging and non-negotiable. According to 1 Corinthians 6:9-10 sexual activity outside of marriage (be it homosexuality, adultery or fornication) will lead ultimately to the loss of salvation. This is the most serious consequence of immorality but there are others. Marriage embodies the heart of God, and unfaithfulness in marriage misrepresents Him.

This does not mean that the Christian message is directed against one group of sinners more than any other. Sin can be defined as a broken relationship with God. The only way to overcome any sinful addiction, whether it be drugs, alcohol, sexual practices or simply selfishness, is to build a relationship with Jesus Christ. Once the door is open for Him then power is available to change the most ingrained habits.

Principle 7: Cultivating a free spirit.

Jesus Christ was the most liberated human being who ever walked the earth. Among His followers the apostle Paul was perhaps the freest man. He was able to move among the most diverse groups of people and identify with them. Being liberated does not mean freedom to indulge in forbidden things. It means simply the freedom from self and sin to the extent that one is free to identify with the needs of others. Paul describes this liberty in Romans 14:15-21

> *"Yet if your brother is grieved because of your food, you are no longer walking in love. Do not destroy with your food the one for whom Christ died. Therefore do not let your good be spoken of as evil; for the kingdom of God is not eating and drinking, but righteousness and peace and joy in the Holy Spirit. For he who serves Christ in these things is acceptable to God and approved by men. Therefore let us pursue the things which make for peace and the things by which one may edify another. Do not destroy the work of God for the sake of food. All things indeed are pure, but it is evil for the man who eats with offense. It is good neither to eat meat nor drink wine nor do anything by which your brother stumbles or is offended or is made weak."*

In this section Paul describes the power of the believer to destroy a brother (verse 15) or even destroy the work of God (verse 20).

Paul is here identifying liberty as not the assertion but the giving up of my rights. This means that liberty is not freedom to indulge but freedom to give up. The great need of leadership is not to promote the rights of any group, but rather to teach all believers to honour one another and to identify with those who are different. If this is applied, then young people in Churches would choose choruses and songs that please older people, while older people would choose songs that please younger ones. The idea that one group of people should insist on singing songs they like is the death knell of the Church. If this be allowed to continue then the Church must fragment.

Illustration: Controversy over baptism stifles a revival
— a story from the life of Charles Finney

Finney in his autobiography describes a great revival in the town of Gouverneur. The revival was stopped when the Baptists began to press the converts to attend their Church and be baptized by immersion. This led to such a controversy that the revival stopped. "The action of the Baptists had the effect of destroying the spirit of prayer and faith, and the work came to a dead stand. For six weeks there was not a single conversion. All, both saints and sinners, were discussing the question of baptism."

Finney then taught on the biblical reasons for believing in baptism by immersion, and then on the next day taught on the biblical reasons for believing in baptism by sprinkling. . "The question was intelligently settled, and soon the people ceased to talk about it. In the course of a few days the spirit of prayer returned, and the revival was revived and went on again with great power. Not long after, the ordinances were administered, and a large number of the converts united with the Church."

Many of us have strong convictions on the subject of baptism, but this will hinder the Spirit of God if we publicly denounce believers who hold to a different interpretation. Adapted from the autobiography of C.G. Finney – chapter 10.

Principle 8: The final absolute: the Day of Judgment.

Many things will change throughout the generations. But of all the unchanging absolutes which we will one day face, the day of judgement is the most fearful. Every human being will one day stand before the judge of the whole earth and give an account for the way they have lived. The citizens of a country are answerable to the tax laws of that country. They may not like them but they will answer to them and they do not have the freedom of creating their own tax structure. One can easily imagine the chaos that would ensue if this were the case. In the same way no human being can escape the final reality of judgment day. The Bible teaches that we will have boldness in the Day of Judgment only if we have a lawyer, an advocate to defend us, and Jesus is that advocate. Those who trust in Him may safely rest their eternal souls in His blood that purchased forgiveness.

"We have an Advocate with the Father, Jesus Christ the righteous. And He Himself is the propitiation for our sins, and not for ours only but also for the whole world." (1 John 2:1-2)

Conclusion:

Christians must beware of being drawn away from the revealed Bible facts to areas of fruitless speculation that water down the message of the Bible. Philosophies and cultures come and go, but the word of God abides forever. At the same time, believers must let go of all that is secondary in order to be soul winners. Winning souls is not just the art of winning unbelievers to Christ; it is the art of winning believers to the joyful unity of the Spirit and all the benefits that follow from that unity.

CHAPTER 10

ACCOUNTABILITY

LEADERSHIP AND ACCOUNTABILITY.

Accountability and the coming of Christ.

Whether we like it or not, every Christian and every minister will one day give an account of their personal life and ministry. We will all give an account of the way we have lived (2 Corinthians 5:10, Romans 14:12, Hebrews 4:13). We will give an account of our casual words as well as our considered statements (Matt 12:36). If we are stewards/leaders we will give an account of our ministry (Luke 16:1-2, Hebrews 13:17). That interview before the judgement seat of Christ will be fearful because there is even the danger that we will be judged with the world. Christ will cut the unjust steward into pieces (Matt 24:45-51). Those who handle their gifts unfaithfully will be cast into outer darkness (Matt 25:30).

There will be rewards and punishments for pastors and leaders. Stewards who acted ignorantly will be punished but less severely than those who acted with knowledge (Luke 12:42-48). Those who built their ministry on wood, hay and straw will find that the day of Christ's coming will both sift and reveal all (1 Corinthians 3:12-15). Many believers will be ashamed at His coming.

Accountability and the danger of losing salvation.

There is often fierce debate about whether it is possible to lose one's salvation. It is right to study the scriptures on this and other vital topics, but the consequences of getting this doctrine wrong are so far reaching. The Bible says that we know in part, and it is right and proper that Christians approach this subject with humility knowing that great men of God have had different views.

One day we will find out who is right, but there could be no greater tragedy than to discover on the last day that we had not lived faithful lives, and that we had forfeited our salvation. Paul himself says that he lived with the awareness that he could be rejected at the end if he lived a careless life:

> *"But I discipline my body and bring it into subjection, lest, when I have preached to others, I myself should become disqualified."*
> *(1 Corinthians 9:27)*

The word "disqualified" is the same word he uses in Titus 1:15-16:

> *"To the pure all things are pure, but to those who are defiled and unbelieving nothing is pure; but even their mind and conscience are defiled. They profess to know God, but in works they deny Him, being abominable, disobedient, and disqualified for every good work."*
> *(Titus 1:15-16)*

The effect of these words by the apostle should be to produce the fear of the Lord in the heart of God's people. This fear of the Lord is not a slavish fear of a tyrant, but rather the fear of loving servants who honour their master and avoid all that would grieve or alienate Him.

Accountability in the course of this life.

The great question is whether ministers should continue for 10, 20, 30 or even 50 years without some measure of accountability. Some ministers may believe that they are unassailable. They are elders/ deacons/pastors/missionaries/Church board members/ preachers etc. and no one has the right to question them re their office or their ministry. This has consequences which may rob the Church in various ways.

Firstly if a minister is failing, there is no way to correct him. Ministers may find that their ministry loses its direction, its freshness and power. At such times they may feel they are trapped in a career with no exit strategy. It may be that a sabbatical may be required to help them re orientate themselves. It may be that there is pressure in the marriage or the wider family that would benefit from a break from the pressures of leadership.

Secondly if he is doing well, but could do better, there is no mechanism to direct him to a better use of his time and gifts. Many ministers are lonely and have no one with whom to discuss the course of life and ministry on which they have embarked. Some ministers may have found themselves doing jobs in the Church for which they are not equipped. Such would greatly benefit from friendly, supportive advice.

Thirdly, some may simply lose hope. There is no worse state of heart than to feel that one is living in vain, that our ministry is having no effect. Ministers need a renewal of perspective to enable them to regain courage for their journey.

Elijah had a tremendous victory on Mount Carmel in 1 Kings 18 but then sank into depression when threatened by Jezebel. He fled for his life:

"But he himself went a day's journey into the wilderness, and came and sat down under a broom tree. And he prayed that he might die, and said, "It is enough! Now, LORD, take my life, for I am no better than my fathers!"
"Then as he lay and slept under a broom tree, suddenly an angel touched him, and said to him, "Arise and eat."
"Then he looked, and there by his head was a cake baked on coals, and a jar of water. So he ate and drank, and lay down again.
And the angel of the LORD came back the second time, and touched him, and said, "Arise and eat, because the journey is too great for you."
(1 Kings 19:4-7)

The angel informed Elijah that the journey was too great for him. The Christian pilgrimage is a marathon not a hundred meter sprint. This is also true for ministers. When people enter into ministry they often have boundless joy and energy believing that they will change the world. The length of our ministry may be long indeed, spanning 50 years or more. Some ministers become cynical and hardened. They continue in their "job" but the dance of joy has departed. The seriousness of this loss of joy is evident in Elijah's prayer that he might be allowed to die. Jonah had this same desire to die when he counselled the crew of the ship to throw him in the sea. This is a deep depression and a solemn loss of hope and it is not rare but is a temptation that will come to many ministers at some point.

To whom might we be accountable?

Many organisations such as WEC and the Anglican Church have mechanisms by which each missionary or pastor will sit for an annual review with other mentors and leaders to see how well they are doing and how they can be helped and encouraged in their ministry. The archbishop of Canterbury sits annually with other leaders to discuss what he is doing well and where he could do better. Sadly structures do not mean that needs are automatically met. True accountability is not something that can easily be organised since it implies a link of openness and trust. Relationships of that kind must be earned and developed over time.

A friend in need is a friend indeed

The real answer is that ministers need a friend. Many ministers have admitted that this was their greatest need throughout their ministry. Most will also confess that this was their most valuable aid in fulfilling their ministry. If friendship is the greatest need of ministers, then they do well to cultivate such bonds. Often people are too busy to give time for this, but it is profitable to deepen friendships through openness and sharing.

What are the qualities of true friendship which will encourage accountability? A true friend is not primarily someone with whom we are very familiar. Many mistake being buddies for being friends. Such a mistake can lead to cronyism, where friends support each other and close ranks to those outside of the close circle. It was said of David:

> *"In that you love your enemies and hate your friends. For you have declared today that you regard neither princes nor servants; for today I perceive that if Absalom had lived and all of us had died today, then it would have pleased you well." (2 Samuel 19:6)*

David was not prejudiced in his opinions in favour of his close friends but expected an unselfish love of others equal to his own.

A friend then is someone who has a deep love for God and His word and will not allow affections to warp their judgment.

> *"Faithful are the wounds of a friend, But the kisses of an enemy are deceitful." (Proverbs 27:6)*

A friend will be faithful even in hard times, when others desert us, and yet still be truthful and gently lead us into paths of faithfulness to Jesus Christ. Jesus Himself is a friend of sinners and yet was able to speak the hardest truth to His closest followers.

Mutual accountability within an eldership.

The best answer and the most biblical manner of answerability is that an eldership will exercise openness and accountability within itself. If openness is lost among the elders it will be quickly discernible by the fact that they find it hard to pray together and may completely abandon doing so. Hebrews 12:15 describes a mutual watchfulness among God's people:

> *"Looking carefully lest anyone fall short of the grace of God; lest any root of bitterness springing up cause trouble, and by this many become defiled." (Hebrews 12:15)*

In the Russian army soldiers are often on patrol or guard duty in sub-zero temperatures. At minus 30 degrees centigrade soldiers cannot feel the effect of frost bite on their face. They are taught to keep a watch on each other and to care for anyone whose skin begins to suffer damage. In the same way leaders are to watch over and pray for one another.

Receiving counsel from mature fathers in the faith

The answer will vary from Church to Church, but ideally a leadership will have received some ministry that has greatly blessed the Church and imparted prophetic direction and faith. There should be more than one ministry that has fathered life and vision in a local assembly. Elders should be encouraged to develop friendships with mature and experienced persons who can provide counsel to individual elders and to groups of elders. An eldership would be wise to develop such relationships in good times so that there will be deep mutual understanding should a crisis situation ever arise. While there may be no need for structure to this relationship, it would nevertheless be wise to make a conscious decision to review the situation of the Church at regular intervals, perhaps once a year. This will aid to relieve pressure from building up and enable a smoother discussion of problems.

It is of vital importance that those who help a leadership never seek to usurp the authority of the local Church. They are counsellors not bureaucrats, helpers not officials. They should shy away from directive advice and help and encourage the answer to rise in the hearts of the leaders themselves.

> *"Counsel in the heart of man is like deep water, But a man of understanding will draw it out." (Proverbs 20:5)*

Accountability to the Church

Ministers are servants in the Church, but the Church is not their master. Moreover the Church is not a democracy but rather a theocracy. Nevertheless leaders are merely members of the Church and as such elderships are to be accountable to the Church and walk step by step with the body of believers. Most leaders will feel no distance between themselves and the Church, and will be aware of the issues in the assembly that are causing joy or concern. Leaders will be approachable and have meaningful fellowship with other members who share a burden for the work of the Lord. If they are out of step with the Church then this will be an area of urgent distress for all. The work of an advisor to the elders is to attend to the personal, spiritual health of the leaders to encourage them to fulfil their ministry. Elders must not engage in a secret agenda and must be open and transparent in matters that affect the whole Church.

So what might accountability look like in practice?

In practice accountability means that an individual minister and a body of elders would be wise to pause and prayerfully reflect on their progress. This should be something that is consciously built into their thinking, and here are a few suggestions about how to action such a process.

1. Don't leave frequency to spontaneity: it would be wise to have a prayerful appraisal on a regular basis. This advice is most relevant for those who are loners and do not easily develop deep and lasting friendships. Many ministers will have friends they contact at regular intervals and develop meaningful relationships. A thorough review every 4-5 years would help a group of elders have confidence they are not facing an endless future without some help. Jim Cymbala commented once in a sermon that he touched base with close friend and mentor Warren Wiersbe once a week.

2. Discretion is the better part of valour! Establishing a framework of accountability is for personal reasons and does not involve public discussion. It is a form of counselling, and the bedrock of counselling is that confidential information is never shared with others. Such a review is unofficial since 'official' can easily become officious! It gives a mechanism for problems to find an expression. If they cannot be solved then at least the pressure of not being able to say anything to anyone is relieved.

3. What kind of questions should one ask either of oneself or of a friend? The following questions may be useful as a starting point for leaders to make a review of their own ministry should they not feel free or able to share with anyone.
   - What is your long term goal for your ministry?
   - Do you feel that you are achieving your goals?

- What is the Lord saying to you at the moment?
- Who can you share with in total openness?
- Who tells you difficult things?
- What are your strengths and weaknesses?
- How can you improve in areas where you are challenged?
- What practical steps can be taken for deepening your prayer life, your Bible reading?
- Are you reading books that expand your spiritual vision and faith?
- What are the main problems in the Church and what is your strategy for solving them?
- E.g. Is the Church growing, and what can be done to help the Church grow?
- Is there a conscious strategy to encourage the younger generation and a passing on of the baton?
- Do you feel that you are forced to do some work that you are not gifted to do: e.g. do you like/dislike admin? Do you like/dislike preaching? Do you like/dislike counselling/visitation?
- Do you think others could be included in the leadership team to take on jobs that you are not doing well and to release you to follow your strengths?
- Is there unity/disunity in the leadership? What are the main problems? E.g. personality clashes? Differences of doctrinal emphasis? Differences of vision?
- Are these problems things that can be resolved, or are they healthy differences that can be allowed to co-exist in a large Church?
- Do you think that you could benefit from some training? Help in preaching style? Getting feedback? Do people think the preaching/meetings are too long, too short?
- Would you benefit from a sabbatical?

Accountability - to what purpose?

- For the affirmation of people in ministry.
- For the benefit of each leader to help them fulfil their ministry leading to the strengthening of local leaderships.
- To help ministers and not to replace them or take authority from them. Any action is taken by the leaders. If there are friends involved from outside they are helping the leadership and are not in authority over them.

When is it right for ministers to move on?

Succession is a difficult issue in many Churches. Some leaders stay too long and others leave too soon! So what are the pitfalls and dangers to avoid?

1. Don't delay to face the issue of succession. A leader should be prayerfully considering this from day one of his ministry. It is right to encourage others to share the burden of the ministry whether or not they will ever be leaders.

2. Do not act by generalisations. Every ministry is unique and each minister must give account to God. Some stay too long and some leave too soon. There is a ripe moment in the timing of God and the leading of the Holy Spirit.

3. Examine your motives for wanting to move. Is it because of a loss of direction, or weariness? If so, then it would be better to give attention to these things first. Faithfulness is the art of sticking at something in hard days as in easy days. Daniel was one of God's faithful servants, and when threatened with death or faithfulness in prayer, he did not hesitate in continuing to pray. (Daniel chapter 6)

4. It has been said that each minister will relate best to his own age group. For this reason it would be good to have a blend of leaders from different generations. As leaders grow older it is wise to appoint younger leaders.

Simple principles of success

1. Learn the principle of joy. We are to serve the Lord with delight. God warned His people of the danger of losing their enjoyment of God and warned that problems would come:

   "Because you did not serve the LORD your God with joy and gladness of heart, for the abundance of everything." (Deuteronomy 28:47)

   If we are not happy in our ministry then it will be communicated unconsciously. Joy is infectious and the Church will sense and partake of the joy of its leaders. George Muller found it a great key to his spiritual life and determined to "keep his soul happy in God."

2. Learn to feed off the Lord and not the Church. Many are so obsessed with how the Church is doing that their moods swing up and down according to how a single meeting goes. Prophets like Daniel and Jeremiah exercised their ministry in very dark days, but found a place of hope that God's plan for Israel would one day triumph in great glory. Find the place of waiting on God and determine never to lose it.

3. Learn the wisdom of a Sabbath rest. Remember that most ministers who suffer burnout do so because they have not built rest into their lives and have paid no attention to delegating responsibility. Find something to help your mind completely switch off from the burdens of responsibility, so that you may be focussed again in your ministry.

4. Remember that we need to be fully rounded people because every Christian minister imparts what he is. The man who does not have any interests outside of the ministry may well find dryness creeping into his soul. "A change is as good as a rest" – which is good advice for the wholeness of our personality. Some activity outside the narrow world of the Church will make our character wholesome and that will help our ministry to be more understanding and relevant. Taking time out with our families will also strengthen the foundations of our relationships and add strength to our whole life.

    There are 4 "fuel tanks" that contribute to the health of every individual. These are:
    1. Emotional 2. Mental 3. Physical and 4. Spiritual.
    Every minister should attend to all four. If we major on the spiritual and neglect the other three, the spiritual side of our life will also wither.

5. Live for Christ not the ministry. The ministry is the revelation of Christ, but if He is not revealed in our character and walk then our preaching will be hollow. Paul did not say "For me to live is preaching" but "For me to live is Christ."

6. Do not allow a false division to arise between leaders and the Church. The priesthood of all believers is a key to the New Covenant concept of ministry. Elitism grieves the Lord, and we are not to yield to this temptation. The line between elders and other Church members is arbitrary. Some people would be leaders of Churches in other contexts, and some elders can have less understanding than some members of the Church.

7. The goal of spiritual leadership is to know God and make Him known. This must always be the focus. We may have plans and projects that we would like to engage in, but the Church is not our place of experimentation. Leaders must not use their authority to push their personal preferences and override others.

Examples of accountability in the New Testament

1. The letters to the seven Churches.

    The clearest example of a review of the work of God in a locality is the second two chapters of Revelation. Here John is given prophetic insight into the spiritual condition of Churches that he knew well. One of the Churches is Ephesus over which he had held responsibility for many years. Jesus was sending this prophetic message to the leaders first: *"to the angel of the Church in Ephesus write."* "Angel" can be translated messenger and probably refers to the leaders of the assembly, (it seems unlikely that Jesus would communicate with angels through the apostles and pen and ink). These blistering messages would have been difficult to receive by some of the leaderships but if taken to heart would have preserved the work of God from terrible calamity.

2. The relationship of Paul with Timothy and Titus.

    There are touching examples of accountability in the letters of Paul to Timothy and Titus. These letters breathe the fragrance of a father's loving and prayerful care of his companions in the ministry. Blessed is the pastor who has a friend like Paul to watch over him and encourage him. All of Paul's letters have elements of this fatherly watchfulness over the Churches. There is not a whiff of bureaucracy or officialdom in Paul's correspondence, nor a desire to control those he is writing to. He is writing as an equal but with a strong burden of affectionate concern.

3. Paul's deference to Peter, James and John.

In Galatians 2:2 Paul seeks the affirmation of his ministry from the apostles Peter, James and John, to ensure that he was not working in vain. In the same chapter Paul describes how on another occasion he was compelled to rebuke Peter for his weakness in caving in to the pressure from the Judaizers (Galatians 2:11). This event illustrates the need for men to be accountable to one another. In this case Peter and Paul were friends and it is probable that they became closer through this event. Peter demonstrated spiritual greatness by receiving the rebuke from Paul with grace. This is implied since there is no evidence that Peter fought back, and later in 2 Peter 3:15-16 Peter commends Paul with deep respect and deference. If Peter had not been able to receive correction then it would have resulted in a deep and painful rift in the Church at Antioch if not all the Churches of the New Testament.

4. Jesus sent out the disciples two by two.

"And He called the twelve to Himself, and began to send them out two by two, and gave them power over unclean spirits." (Mark 6:7)

"After these things the Lord appointed seventy others also, and sent them two by two before His face into every city and place where He Himself was about to go." (Luke 10:1)

Jesus sent His servants out in twos. Paul went with Barnabas on his first missionary journey in obedience to prophetic guidance (Acts 13:2) and with Silas on his second (Acts 15:40). He gladly received others including Timothy (Acts 16:1-3) and Luke (assumed by the use of "we" in Acts 16:11). It is easy for men to be loners and to work in such isolation that they become cut off from correction or encouragement. But the greatest benefit of working with others is in the realm of safeguards to guard against temptations. The New Testament presents strong evidence that Churches were led by more than one man and often by a group in close fellowship as can be seen in Antioch in Acts 13:1-3.

Accountability in Moral behaviour.

It is of supreme importance that leaders uphold the highest standards of personal moral behaviour. This is because they are preaching the kingdom of God which has the highest standards of moral and spiritual excellence. For this reason no one in the Church should engage in private counselling without total adherence to the highest code of conduct. Some ministers are naive and assume that others with whom they are involved share the same moral standards. This is not the case, and for this reason the following guidelines should be fully grasped and implemented.

1. Avoid all appearance of evil. (1 Thessalonians 5:22).

    No one should ever be alone with a member of the opposite sex. This is to avoid temptation, but it will also avoid false accusations. If there is a witness to our conduct then that will be an invaluable aid in handling an accusation.

2. Avoid emotional dependence.

    Pastors are not to allow members to become emotionally

dependent. A pastor may find that he is admired by a young woman who enjoys his authority and interest in her life. She may approach him for advice and counsel. The minister must gently refuse to help in such circumstances and attach the girl to a female worker. Such relationships are out of place, and may be because of deep hurts in the individual's past. It may for example be the absence of a father that has left the individual with a need for emotional support. While such scenarios may be rare, leaders must build their conduct on keeping emotional detachment from those they are seeking to help. Jesus Christ loved His disciples with a pure love that was not emotionally intense or exclusive. Emotional detachment does not mean the absence of love; it rather defines the purity of that love.

3. Avoid intense or exclusive relationships of any kind.

Leaders must avoid all male/female relationships that are intense or exclusive. Men and women must work together in groups. It is naive in the extreme to assume that human passions will always remain absent. Some mistakenly speak of platonic relationships and will meet for Bible study or spiritual discussion. This is folly and may well end in disaster. Exclusive male/female friendships are to be developed solely in the context of marriage. Some pastors will have co-workers in the Church's administrative structure such as secretaries or youth leaders. Great wisdom is required to develop working structures and an environment in which temptation is avoided.

4. Understanding the difference between moral indiscretion and criminal acts.

If a pastor receives an accusation against a member of the Church he is to understand that this may well be beyond his competency. If an accusation concerns an inappropriate relationship such as adultery, the Church will have to handle the matter with firmness and biblical discipline. However, if the accusation concerns sexual abuse, whether child abuse, or misuse of authority to coerce a sexual favour, then this is a case of criminal activity and must involve the police and the law courts. This may well be a painful course of action especially if it involves friends whose lives will be damaged by such exposure. It is easy to have one's judgment clouded by the pressure of very serious consequences. However the action of covering up such activity is in itself criminal and can only make things worse in the long run. Some may object that Christians are to forgive and not to pursue things before worldly courts. It is true that forgiveness is vital but this does not mean that a person may escape the consequences of their crimes. Imagine the worst cases of murder and child abuse. The victims need to forgive their assailant, but that does not mean their attacker should escape a prison sentence.

5.   Financial accountability.

Money is given to missions and Churches on trust. There can be no reason why accounts should be kept secret from the Church members. Such secrecy may rightly produce a sense of unease among donors. A lack of transparency may stray into a breach of criminal law.

Conclusion

Accountability is to be achieved through meaningful friendships among God's servants. Such friendships will keep ministers in paths of righteousness, holiness and humility. Jesus sent out disciples two by two. Going it alone may be an attractive ideal to some, but it is a dangerous path that can lead to deep problems.

.

CHAPTER 11

THE PREACHING MINISTRY

A. The need to declare God's truth

"We will give ourselves continually to prayer and to the ministry of the word." (Acts 6:4)

Not all leaders are preachers. But all leaders are to understand some of the principles of preaching. The apostles said in Acts 6:4 that they would give themselves to this ministry. This also implied that the seven deacons would not give themselves in the same measure to this ministry. It is important that each member of the Church have the liberty to be themselves. For those who are not called to preach, they are to understand the importance of this ministry and pray for it.

"Praying ... for me, that utterance may be given to me, that I may open my mouth boldly to make known the mystery of the gospel."
(Ephesians 6:19)

The preaching ministry is of vital importance to the growth and health of the Church. The word of God is God's method of reaching the hearts of believers and unbelievers. Preaching is distinct from lecturing. In a lecture, facts are presented in a manner which reaches the mind. Preaching should always address the reasoning faculty especially at the outset. But it must progress to reach the heart addressing primarily the conscience and the will.

Paul said:

> *"For since, in the wisdom of God, the world through wisdom did not know God, it pleased God through the foolishness of preaching to save those who believe." (1 Corinthians 1:21)*

Preaching in the post-modern era.

The post-modern world rejects absolutes whether religious or moral. People now do not wait to be told what to do; they wait to be engaged in discussion. The mind-set of the 21st century does not want to be instructed about the universe, but to help to form its own. This is the opposite of the preaching ministry, which declares the truth of God and demands response. No matter how unpopular, the Church must not compromise on the preaching ministry, after all their Lord and Master Jesus was and is Himself a preacher. Churches may have many programmes, but they cannot substitute anything for the preaching ministry. They may be involved in social action, and perhaps run hospitals or schools, but none of these can ever be a substitute for the Word of God being preached. Even counselling, Alpha courses, etc. cannot replace God's chosen method of having truth declared.

The Greek words for preaching are:

♦ **_Evangelizo_.** This means to give good news. Not all that a preacher says will be in itself good. A preacher will have to bring his hearers to recognise they are sinners, but the overwhelming good news is that God has found a solution to the awful condition of sinners alienated from a Holy God.

♦ **_Kerusso_.** To herald the truth of the kingdom, the greatness of God, the power of the cross. The herald goes before the king and declares the imminent arrival of the king, who is following behind. John the Baptist was the King's herald – he opened the door for Jesus. The preacher is a herald who opens the door for Jesus to enter the lives and situations of the people.

B. Essential foundations of the preaching ministry

1. The Baptism with the Holy Spirit

The Lord commanded His apostles not to go into all the world until they were endued with power from on high (Luke 24:49; Acts 1:8). The baptism with the Holy Spirit made the apostles witnesses of the supreme victory of the cross. It made them witnesses of Christ and of His death and resurrection, because it united them with the power of the cross. Many people have known the incredible transformation of their ministry through the baptism with the Holy Spirit.

****

The testimony of D.L. Moody

D.L. Moody was a successful minister but, by his own admission later, he lacked the power in his ministry. One day two women came up to him after a service. They said, "We have been praying for you." "Why don't you pray for the people?" he asked. "Because you need the power of the Spirit", they said. "I need the power! Why", said Moody, in relating the incident years after, "I thought I had power. I had the largest congregations in Chicago, and there were many conversions."

Moody also said that, in a sense, he was satisfied. He was in a comfort zone. But these two praying women rocked the boat. They told him that they were praying for an anointing by the Holy Spirit for him to have a special service to God. He could not get this off his mind and he said, "There came a great hunger in my soul. I did not know what it was and I began to cry out to God as never before. I felt I did not want to live if I could not have this power for service".

After the great fire of Chicago, Moody was working to raise money to rebuild a tabernacle. He said his heart was not in it because he kept crying out to God to fill him. During a visit to New York to raise money, he withdrew and prayed; he cried that God would fill him with His Spirit. He described it this way: "Well, one day, in the city of New York -- oh, what a day! -- I cannot describe it, I seldom refer to it; it is almost too sacred an experience to name. Paul had an experience of which he never spoke for 14 years. I can only say that God revealed Himself to me, and I had such an experience of His love that I had to ask Him to stay His hand. I went to preaching again. The sermons were not different; I did not present any new truths, and yet hundreds were converted. I would not now be placed back where I was before that blessed experience if you should give me all the world -- it would be as the small dust of the balance."

****

The baptism with the Holy Spirit makes us witnesses not just when we are preaching but also when we are living. Jesus said: *"You shall **be** witnesses to Me"* (Acts 1:8). By the baptism with the Spirit, there is power without striving, because it is the grace and power of God at work.

2. The Messenger is also the Message

The preacher and the message must be one. The preacher is ministering concerning someone greater than himself, but he is a channel and he must be pure. Just as we want to drink pure water from a clean cup, so too we must hear the gospel through clean vessels. It is true that God can use even a donkey, but this is not His chosen method! The preacher will impart his own heart state; this impacts the hearers when they hear preaching. They can tell if the preacher is in faith, fear, unbelief or frustration. A congregation can soon tell if the preacher is a hard or a loving person. If the preacher talks about something he has not experienced, the congregation will soon realise this. If he is preaching about the baptism with the Holy Spirit, then obviously he must be full of the Holy Spirit.

Every voice is from a spirit: either God's, man's or Satan's. When we preach we minister the states of our own hearts in some measure. This is why we must make sure that we are in communion with God, and that we are speaking and ministering the knowledge of God. If we are in gross sin in our hearts, God will not allow us to continue in the ministry. He will not have hypocrites representing His kingdom.

4. Judgment Begins at the House of God
...and with the Preachers

Peter explains that, when Christ returns, judgment must begin at the house of God (1 Peter 4:17). Christ describes the Day of Judgment in Matthew 24:42–25:46. He begins by explaining that the first people to be judged will be the servants of His house.

The word He uses for His 'house' (Luke 12:42 and Matthew 24:45) is *"therapeia,"* which can be taken to mean 'house of healing'. The Church is intended to be a place of healing of wounds; but Jesus describes some servants as inflicting wounds on others (Matthew 24:49). Preachers can inflict wounds on their hearers. Jesus said that the scribes (or lawyers) laid burdens on people that were heavy for them to bear (Matthew 23:4; Luke 11:46). He also said that such servants who wound others will be dismembered or cut into pieces when He returns (Matthew 24:51)!

Plainly, Jesus views the preaching ministry as very important.
As James says:

> *"...let not many of you become teachers, knowing that we shall receive a stricter judgment"* (James 3:1).

Jesus said that if we break the least commandment and teach others to do so, we shall be called least in the Kingdom of Heaven (Matthew 5:19). Clearly it is an awesome act to stand before people and teach them the ways of God, and His word.

Jesus said in Matthew 24:45 that faithful servants are those who feed His flock the right food in the right season. This means that preachers must discern the right food for the flock, and not repeat their favourite topics! On at least three occasions elders/pastors are exhorted to feed (or shepherd) the flock of God (John 21:15-17; Acts 20:28; 1 Peter 5:2). The food of the flock is clearly the Word; but this cannot mean mere Bible knowledge, or professors would be the best pastors. Jesus reveals to Peter that the food of the flock is available when a pastor truly loves Him. Jesus did not want to know how much time Peter spent in prayer or how much of the Scriptures he read daily. He asked Peter if he loved Him. If we love Jesus, we will have food for the flock and we will minister healing to the flock as we feed them.

4. The Released Preacher Must First be Released in Prayer

Preaching is not to be a lecture. It is an interaction between God and people to declare the truth of God. There is of necessity a prophetic dimension to preaching. Not that the word 'prophecy' is the New Testament word for preaching - this would require a strained interpretation of the word 'prophecy'. But the prophetic element in preaching is the declaration of the hidden things of God and the secret thoughts of the hearers. When there is true preaching, congregations feel searched by the word, and exposed under the searching eye of God.

For this kind of preaching to take place, the preacher must be filled with the Holy Spirit and also released or abandoned to the Holy Spirit. Some preachers are too 'controlled' - they rely totally on their minds and are never prepared to be spontaneous. The preacher must be gripped by God if he is to lay hold of a congregation by his preaching. The place where this happens is in prayer. The preacher must let go of himself in worship. He does not become mindless, but he does not remain a slave to intellectualism. He knows the place of worship and of communion with God. Paul says that he knew what it was to be *'beside himself'* and what it was to be sober or *'of sound mind' (2 Corinthians 5:13).* The faculty of reason must kneel humbly while the spirit soars in worship. There are aspects of preaching that are communicated when a preacher soars with the Holy Spirit. They cannot be manufactured, but they can be prepared by quiet waiting on God, and adoring worship.

5. The Call of God

The greatest calling that a person can ever have is the one God intended for them! It is possible for the preaching ministry to be exalted over all other gifts and ministries. However, it is not possible to *choose* to be a preacher, any more than it is possible to choose to have a prophetic ministry etc. This is God's choice. Martyn Lloyd-Jones said that if you ever meet a man who claims to be called to the ministry' do everything you can to make it hard for him! While few of us will unreservedly agree with Dr Jones on this point, it is nevertheless important to realise that true preachers have come through all discouragements and struggles, to the place where they can fulfil their ministry, overcoming obstacles in order to be a preacher.

- **Each person must know their calling**: Martyn Lloyd-Jones tells of a man who was a car mechanic but left his work to train as a pastor. He was happy until he went into the ministry, at which point he lost all his joy. He continued on for several years until he realised that God had not called him to the ministry. As soon as he realised this, he returned to his calling as a mechanic and found his joy again.

- **What is the call?** This is difficult to put into words, but it is not a natural gift, even though it does in some measure flow with natural gifts. Although someone with a stammer and a poor grasp of language may be used by God, it is nevertheless true that most preachers have good communication ability. This is the case in the examples of Peter, Stephen, Paul and others in the New Testament. Their ability to speak was not the call of God, but it enabled them to fulfil their calling. The call, then, is an inner compulsion. Paul said:

"For if I preach the gospel, I have nothing to boast of, for necessity is laid upon me; yes, woe is me if I do not preach the gospel! For if I do this willingly, I have a reward; but if against my will, I have been entrusted with a stewardship. What is my reward then? That when I preach the gospel, I may present the gospel of Christ without charge, that I may not abuse my authority in the gospel." (1 Corinthians 9:16-18)

It must be added that Paul's preaching was not *"with excellence of speech or of wisdom" (1 Corinthians 2:1)*. His enemies said his speech was *"contemptible" (2 Corinthians 10:10)*. Paul's gift was extraordinary in its power and effect, and it was by no means a natural gift.

- **The call surpasses every other demand on our life**: when Peter and John heard the call, they left all and followed Jesus. The call was that if they would follow Him, He would make them fishers of men (Mark 1:17). This does not mean that every called person must leave their employment. But it does mean that when someone is conscious of the call, they must let go of everything that competes with it. Paul said that he had suffered the loss of all things in pursuit of the call to know Christ (Philippians 3:7-14). The call is not primarily to a ministry, but to a person, whom we are to love and enjoy.

- **We are called to minister to God first and to people second**: Jesus said that the first commandment is to love God and the second commandment is to love our neighbour as ourselves (Mark 12:29-31). Often ministry is person-centred or need-centred. But Jesus did not minister to needs first; He ministered to Father first, and the outflow of His obedience to the Father was that people's needs were abundantly met. But Jesus did not follow the pressure of need; He followed the guidance of His Father. Even as He left the upper room to go to Gethsemane and the cross, He declared that He was doing it because He loved the Father.

When we get overwhelmed with need, as we surely must if we concentrate on human problems, we become dry and unable to help anyone. We must concentrate on enjoying and pleasing God. Paul said that if he were a people-pleaser he would not be a servant of Christ (Galatians 1:10). When Elijah went to the widow of Zarephath, he told her to make cakes for him first, and then for her son and herself (1 Kings 17:13). This contradicted the obvious need that she had, but the result was that her needs were met in a much more glorious way than could ever have happened if she had put her own needs first. Ministers must take time to sit at the feet of Jesus, listening to Him and to His word, if they are to be effective.

6. Preach Christ and Him Crucified

When the New Testament speaks of the apostles' preaching ministry, it uses strange grammar. Paul says he had resolved to *"preach Christ crucified"* (1 Corinthians 1:23, 2:2). The apostles did not cease *"teaching and preaching Jesus Christ"* (Acts 5:42). The normal grammar would indicate that they taught 'about' Jesus Christ. But clearly it is not within the bounds of normal grammar to explain what happens during the act of preaching.

When a preacher declares the person and work of Christ, the person of Christ should be manifest during the preaching. Paul says in Titus 1:3 that God *"has manifested His word through preaching"*. Because Christ is raised from the dead and present everywhere, then during the true ministry of preaching, congregations should be conscious of God. They should sense the presence of Jesus. He should reach out through the preaching and touch the lives of people present. The preacher himself is to be invisible, as Christ is made manifest. For this to take place, the preacher must himself have fully embraced his own death, so that he is dead to self. It does not mean that he is always apologetic or embarrassed standing in front of people. The person who is truly free from self is free to be confident before congregations; he is not self-conscious at all. He is God-conscious and is liberated to flow in the Holy Spirit. Embarrassment is the sign that we are not free from self!

The preacher is then fully aware that, though there may be many important subjects to preach about - such as the Second Coming, marriage, the Tabernacle, marketplace ethics etc. yet there is only one theme that grips him as the supreme key to the problems that people face. That one subject is Christ and His cross. The Holy Spirit loves Jesus and is in holy awe about the cross. Therefore, when a preacher talks about these things, the Holy Spirit is filled with holy wonder, and applies them to the hearts of the hearers.

People have created audio and video recording equipment that can replay moments in history. But the greatest recorder of all is the Holy Spirit. He recorded the creation as it took place. He is the witness to the deep things of God, including the cross, and it is through Him alone that these things are made known (1 Corinthians 2:4-10). It is through the preaching of Christ that He is made known.

C. The snares of the preaching ministry

The mark of the true ministry is holiness, and a lifestyle that demonstrates the fruit of the Spirit. Jesus said there would be false prophets, but that we would know them by their fruits (Matthew 7:15-23). Similarly, the marks of the false prophets in Jude and 2 Peter 2, are that they do not resist temptation, but give in to sin.

There are many snares to the preaching ministry; here are the three main ones that are emphasised in the New Testament:

1. Pride and the Idolatry of the Ministry

Some preachers get a buzz from preaching. They enjoy the thrill of being the centre of attention and enjoy holding the congregation in their control through the power of their preaching. It can become like a drug that they cannot live without. Paul said: *"woe is me if I do not preach the gospel!"* (1 Corinthians 9:16), but he was not referring to his own enjoyment of the ministry, but to the divine compulsion to do the will of God. He said, *"for me to live is Christ"* - not preaching (Philippians 1:21). He was content in prison because preaching was not his life, but knowing Jesus was. If we fall into this temptation we will become arrogant and proud, possibly falling into other equally serious sins.

2. The Love of Money – the Sin of Balaam and Gehazi
(2 Peter 2:15-16; Jude 11)

Balaam preached and prophesied hoping for financial reward (Numbers 22-24). Gehazi took Naaman's money and contracted Naaman's leprosy (2 Kings 5:20-27). Not all preachers will find big financial rewards in preaching, but this temptation can arise for all successful preachers. The preacher must not have an eye on the gift he is hoping to receive after the sermon. (Few treasurers will hand over a gift at the beginning of a service or weekend of ministry!) If our preaching is powerful, some people may be delivered or healed, and wish to express their gratitude by giving large gifts. If the preacher mentions his financial needs in the preaching, it is possible that wealthy members of the congregation will want to help him. The preacher must trust God for his support, and not manipulate congregations to give him money. This will require great self-control on occasions. When a rich person asks a preacher with no money in his pocket if there is anything he needs, the preacher must answer faithfully, and not exploit the generosity of the believers.

There is no such thing as a 'poor' preacher. Even if the preacher has no money, he must never complain that he is poor! Imagine telling someone, *"I'm poor, I only have Jesus!"* It would be like a billionaire's wife complaining that she had no money of her own, just her husband to rely on! The preacher has all the resources of Jesus Christ at his disposal, and Jesus will give him whatever he needs and never too late.

Kathryn Kuhlman gave generously to David Wilkerson, so he loved to go and minister at her services knowing that she would give generously to Teen Challenge. After some years, the Holy Spirit showed him that he had been relying on her and not on God. So he learned to go there only when he felt it was the will of God. Some people have made great sacrifices to be preachers, but if they have little money in their pocket, it can be tempting to let it be known that they do not have enough money for a holiday or a car. This can be expressed in a way that dishonours God, who is their employer!

> *One English vicar took the Anglican Church to court, claiming that his pay was too low. The judge wisely dismissed the case, on the grounds that the man's employer was God and therefore beyond the competence of the court!*

3. Immorality

Preachers are targets of the devil. If he can make preachers fall then he can ruin their ministry. Proverbs 6:26 teaches us that, *"the adulteress seeks the precious life"*. There can be no doubt that the devil rejoices when precious servants of God fall into immorality. Proverbs 6:32–33 teaches that whoever commits adultery *"destroys his own soul"* and *"his shame will never be wiped away"*. We may argue, *"Is there no forgiveness for such sins?"* Of course there is forgiveness, and restoration to salvation and fellowship with God and with His people. But the ministry of such men will be permanently damaged; never again will they be able to minister without someone remembering their sin.

Preachers (and ordinary believers) should resolve never to be alone in a compromising situation. They should refuse to be alone with a member of the opposite sex. They should refuse to counsel a member of the opposite sex alone, but should seek support from their spouse or other counsellors.

Churches, and particularly preachers, are **targets of the prince of darkness**. In the 1980s it was reported that a band of witches in South Africa had undertaken a 40-day fast to Satan with the intention of destroying Christian marriages.

CONCLUSION: The Lord's servants must care for their own hearts, to make sure they are walking with the Lord in a healthy spiritual state, able to resist the temptations of the wicked one.

D. Five spiritual keys for preachers:

1. Pray as Much as You Read in Preparation

It is a sad fact that many people trust in the reputation of the preacher, or in his gifts and experience or Bible knowledge. None of these can save anyone. It is only the Holy Spirit Who can take our preaching and make it powerful and effective.

Read the following example about the conversion of Spurgeon, in his own words. When he went to a certain chapel, the preacher was unable to get there because of a heavy snowfall. The preacher who took his place was not naturally gifted, but God used him mightily.

****

I sometimes think I might have been in darkness and despair until now, had it not been for the goodness of God in sending a snowstorm one Sunday morning, while I was going to a certain place of worship. When I could go no further, I turned down a side street, and came to a little Primitive Methodist Chapel. In that chapel there may have been a dozen or fifteen people. I had heard of the Primitive Methodists, how they sang so loudly that they made people's heads ache; but that did not matter to me. I wanted to know how I might be saved, and if they could tell me that, I did not care how much they made my head ache. The minister did not come that morning; he was snowed up, I suppose. At last, a very thin-looking man, a shoemaker, or tailor, or something of that sort, went up into the pulpit to preach. Now, it is well that preachers should be instructed; but this man was really stupid. He was obliged to stick to his text, for the simple reason that he had little else to say. The text was:
"LOOK UNTO ME, AND BE YE SAVED, ALL THE ENDS OF THE EARTH."
He did not even pronounce the words rightly, but that did not matter. There was, I thought, a glimpse of hope for me in that text. The preacher began thus— "My dear friends, this is a very simple text indeed. It says, 'Look'. Now lookin'

don't take a deal of pains. It ain't liftin' your foot or your finger; it is just, 'Look'.

Well, a man needn't go to College to learn to look. Anyone can look; even a child can look. But then the text says, 'Look unto Me'. Ay!" said he, in broad Essex, "many on ye are lookin' to yourselves, but it's no use lookin' there. You'll never find any comfort in yourselves. Some look to God the Father. No, look to Him by-and-by. Jesus Christ says, 'Look unto Me'. Some on ye say, 'We must wait for the Spirit's workin'. You have no business with that just now. Look to Christ. The text says, 'Look unto Me'."

Then the good man followed up his text in this way: "Look unto Me; I am sweatin' great drops of blood. Look unto Me; I am hangin' on the cross. Look unto Me; I am dead and buried. Look unto Me; I rise again. Look unto Me; I ascend to Heaven. Look unto Me; I am sittin' at the Father's right hand. O poor sinner, look unto Me, look unto Me!"

When he had gone to about that length, and managed to spin out ten minutes or so, he was at the end of his tether. Then he looked at me under the gallery, and I daresay, with so few present, he knew me to be a stranger. Just fixing his eyes on me, as if he knew all my heart, he said, "Young man, you look very miserable." Well, I did; but I had not been accustomed to have remarks made from the pulpit on my personal appearance before. However, it was a good blow, struck right home. He continued, "and you always will be miserable—miserable in life, and miserable in death,—if you don't obey my text; but if you obey now, this moment, you will be saved." Then, lifting up his hands, he shouted, as only a Primitive Methodist could do, "Young man, look to Jesus Christ. Look! Look! Look! You have nothin' to do but to look and live."

I saw at once the way of salvation. I know not what else he said—I did not take much notice of it—I was so possessed with that one thought. Like as when the brazen serpent was lifted up, the people only looked and were healed, so it was with me. I had been waiting to do fifty things, but when I heard that word, "Look!" what a charming word it seemed to me! Oh! I looked until I could almost have looked my eyes away. There and then the cloud was gone, the darkness had rolled away, and that moment I saw the sun; and I could have risen that instant, and sung with the most enthusiastic of them, of the precious blood of Christ, and the simple faith which looks alone to Him. Oh, that somebody had told me this before, "Trust Christ, and you shall be saved."

****

The point of the story is that God uses a power that is wholly greater than us. If we rely on God, we will pray more and look to Him to work rather than to ourselves.

2. Be Bold in the Lord

After the lame beggar had been healed at the Beautiful Gate of the Temple, Peter was very bold when he was taken before the Sanhedrin (Acts 4:8-13). He was not boastful about his gifts and abilities, but he was very bold in proclaiming the person of Jesus Christ.

3. Rely on the Holy Spirit

After the lame beggar was healed, Peter said to all the people who ran to him and John:

"...why (do you) look so intently at us, as though by our own power or godliness we had made this man walk?" (Acts 3:12)

Peter was quick to let them know that it wasn't himself and John who had healed the man, but Jesus. He took it a step further, to say it wasn't even his faith, but the faith that comes from Jesus (Acts 3:16). Peter was not afraid to let people know that he was weak without God.

4. Soak in the Bible Passage You Want to Preach from

Prayerfully read and re-read the text and context — both in English and in the original (use as many translations as possible).

G. Campbell Morgan said that, before he preached from a passage in any book of the Bible, he read that entire book 50 times. If we give the true sense of the Bible we will be deep preachers, because the Bible is a deep book. It brings to light hidden truths about God and human beings. We will be the best psychologists, the best philosophers, the best counsellors, if we stick to what the Bible says.

5. Challenge the Hearts of the People

A preacher is not speaking to people's heads only, but also to their hearts. Peter had something to say that would change people's lives, so he said: *"... heed my words"* (Acts 2:14). We must be challenging. Information is needed, but it must be given in a way that can be applied in people's lives.

"... we ought to give the more earnest heed to the things which we have heard, lest at any time we should let them slip" (Hebrews 2:1)

If people don't heed the word preached, they could easily let the truth of God's word slip away from them.

"... faith by itself, if it does not have works, is dead" (James 2:17)

"For indeed the gospel was preached to us as well as to them; but the word which they heard did not profit them, not being mixed with faith in those who heard it." (Hebrews 4:2)

People will not profit from our ministry unless we get them to put the Word into practice. The Bible says we are to *"consider one another in order to stir up love and good works" (Hebrews 10:24).*

188

E. Ten practical keys

(1) Know what you want the people to do after they have heard you preach.

Do you want the people:

- To repent, believe and be saved?
- To receive the baptism with the Holy Spirit?
- To be prayed with for healing or deliverance?
- To worship God?
- To receive greater understanding and take time to digest the new insights you have ministered to them?

You should have a clear object in mind if you want to be effective. You might change your objective during your preaching if the Holy Spirit leads you to do so. But you should have a clear objective in mind from the moment you start speaking.

(2) Be clear - don't keep big surprises for the end of your sermon

Tell people what you are going to talk about, then talk about it, then tell them what you have talked about! Repetition is the art of the good communicator. Make sure you have communicated your main message. Ask yourself, "What are the main things I want people to remember from this message?"

(3) Don't use big words when you can use small ones

Speak so that a ten-year-old can understand you. That is what Billy Graham intended. If you have been to Bible College and studied the Greek and the Hebrew, this is a great advantage in understanding the Bible. But it is no use trying to dazzle congregations with your great knowledge! Peter spoke Hebrew, Aramaic and Greek fluently, as they were his native languages. But he could not understand the Saviour because of his spiritual dullness, and needed to have things spelt out to him (Mark 8:14-21). Most people need things to be expressed simply.

(4) Make a clear outline with:

- ♦ An introduction
- ♦ Your main points, with examples
- ♦ Your conclusion
- ♦ Your appeal or challenge to the will of your hearers

(5) Study

"Be diligent to present yourself approved to God, a worker who does not need to be ashamed, rightly dividing the word of truth" (2 Timothy 2:15)

There are certain Bible tools that will help the preacher. They are not expensive, and are useful in widening our understanding of the Scriptures. (e.g. Halley's Bible Handbook, Unger's Bible Dictionary, Strong's Concordance, Vine's Dictionary, *Explore the Book* by Sidlow Baxter).

(6) Memorise the Scriptures

There is nothing more powerful than the Word of God. Peter, in his sermon on the Day of Pentecost, quoted large sections of Scripture. He knew them by heart. God has given the promise that His word will not return to Him void (Isaiah 55:10-11). It is sharper than any two-edged sword (Hebrews 4:12). The word will do more in the hearts of people than a preacher ever can.

(7) Use your voice to the full but don't scream - Peter *"raised his voice"* (Acts 2:14). But this does not mean that he was screaming! Once, a small child asked, *"Why is the pastor so mad at us"*, referring to the preacher. Equally, we must not use a monotonous voice that will make people go to sleep. Once, a young preacher screamed at the congregation, *"We need sermons that will awaken the Church!"* A wise old pastor was sitting behind him and said, loud enough to be heard, *"What we first need are sermons that don't put people to sleep!"*

(8) Don't rely on tricks to get effect

You may use illustrations, but be careful not to undermine your ministry by play-acting. While we may be dramatic in our preaching, we must not pretend.

> *Campbell Morgan tells of an American businessman who went to hear a preacher in the Eastern USA. During his preaching, the preacher stopped and said: "I can't quite find the right word.... Perhaps it is... or ..." and then he found the right word. The businessman was impressed with the spontaneous manner in which the preacher spoke. Three weeks later he was in the West Coast of USA and had the opportunity to hear the preacher again. During his preaching, the preacher stopped and said: "I can't quite find the right word... Perhaps it is... or..." The businessman suddenly realised that the man had not been spontaneous at all but had been play-acting! He left the meeting in disgust.*

(9) Beware of humour

Preachers are not to be comedians, especially if you want the congregation to take you seriously. Some preachers use humour to 'soften up' their congregation. This may sometimes be necessary if there is tension in the congregation. Humour may help you and the congregation relax, but beware! It will be hard to connect with the atmosphere of the Spirit and of heaven if we lose ourselves in carnal laughter. Jesus and the apostles did not tell jokes, though there is little doubt that God has a sense of humour. Jesus would have laughed along with everybody else at life's humorous situations.

(10) Know when to stop

The truth is that few preachers know when to stop, especially when they really get warmed up to their subject.

A little boy went to Church with his father. When the preacher came in he placed a Bible, a notebook and a watch on the pulpit. "What are those for?" asked the little boy. "Well", said the father, the Bible is the Word of God; the notebook is the outline of what the preacher wants to say to us, and the watch? Well, the watch doesn't mean anything at all!"

Sometimes the preacher is not connecting with the congregation, so he may talk on and on, trying to connect. Others have a great connection but do not know when to stop. Remember these guidelines:

- If you drill for oil and don't find it within 15 minutes, stop boring!

- Always leave a congregation wishing you had spoken longer, rather than wishing you had stopped sooner.

- Always remember that some of your congregation have been working hard all week and will be struggling to keep their concentration. You may not be tired, but they may be exhausted.

- Listening is sometimes a harder discipline than speaking! Remember moments when you wanted the preacher to stop.

- There will be a ripe moment to stop. If you miss it, the message of the Holy Spirit may be forgotten. People will be ready to respond, but if you miss the moment, they may be discouraged.

- Honour the congregation and the leaders, even if you are the leader of the Church! Remember that finishing on time will help Sunday School leaders.

Conclusion.

The preaching ministry is the context in which the mind of the Church is shaped.

"For as a man thinks in his heart, so he is." (Proverbs 23:7)

If the mind is healthy and strong then the Church will also be healthy and strong. For this end the preacher must give himself to the prayerful study of God's word so that his preaching will produce the mind of Christ in himself and his hearers. This is a high calling and preachers must set a high goal for themselves since they serve the great King to whom they must give account.

CHAPTER 12

THE ROLE OF WOMEN

A Glass Slipper to fit all sizes?

It was not my intention to write about the role of women when I started writing this book. However it is an unavoidable background question that arises at many points as the subject of leadership is examined. This book also has the impossible task of being like a shoe (or glass slipper!) that fits all sizes, since it will be read by believers from different backgrounds.

In some Churches, women take a very prominent role already and many will be puzzled why it is a question at all. Others will be from a background in which women have a very small role, and are excluded from senior positions in the Church. Moreover in many Churches there will be a senior pastor who will have a board of elders and/or deacons. In other Churches there will be a board of elders leading the Church, while few Churches have the office of an "apostle." This means that the definition of the words "apostle," "elder" and "deacon" will also vary from Church to Church. The whole question of defining the roles of these three offices is like trying to hit a moving target. To make the task even more difficult the role of women in the Church varies through the changing generations and geographical cultures of the world. Readers in Asia, South and North America, Africa and Europe will have a totally different cultural take on this subject.

God wants men and women to be fully active in the life and ministry of the Church:

"The Lord gives the word; the women who announce the news are a great host," Psalm 68:11 ESV.

This verse was used in Handel's Messiah where it is translated:

"The Lord gave the word; great was the company of the preachers." KJV

The Hebrew word for preachers is in the feminine form.

"And it shall come to pass in the last days, says God, That I will pour out of My Spirit on all flesh; Your sons and your daughters shall prophesy, Your young men shall see visions, Your old men shall dream dreams. And on My menservants and on My maidservants I will pour out My Spirit in those days; And they shall prophesy." (Acts 2:17-18 NKJV)

From these two verses alone there can be no doubt that God expects women to be involved in the ministry of God's word. This is revolutionary for some Churches that have not allowed women to participate freely in Church life. That women can prophesy is simply a Bible fact. There were many prophetesses in the Old Testament, including Miriam (Exodus 15:20), Deborah (Judges 4:4), Huldah (2 Kings 22:14), Noadiah (Nehemiah 6:14) and Isaiah's unnamed wife (Isaiah 8:3). Despite the male dominated nature of the culture of those days, women played a major role in the spiritual life of the nation.

In the New Testament, God spoke prophetically through Mary the mother of Jesus, and Elizabeth the mother of John the Baptist. Anna was a prophetess (Luke 2:36) and Philip had four daughters who prophesied (Acts 21:9).

The main principles regarding the roles of men and women.

There are many principles that will shape our understanding of the different roles of men and women in the Church. Here are five that will help local assemblies understand God's will and purpose.

Principle 1 - The Attitude of Christ to women
Principle 2 - Men must bear the burden of responsibility
Principle 3 - Women may exercise spiritual authority
Principle 4 - Men and women have different roles
Principle 5 - Every Church family is unique

Once these biblical principles are established they will provide a framework to answer the specific questions on the role of women.

Principle 1 - The Attitude of Christ to women

> *"Perhaps it is no wonder that the women were first at the Cradle and last at the Cross. They had never known a man like this Man - there never has been such another. A prophet and teacher who never nagged at them, never flattered or coaxed or patronized; who never made arch jokes about them, never treated them either as "The women, God help us!" or "The ladies, God bless them!"; who rebuked without querulousness and praised without condescension; who took their questions and arguments seriously; who never mapped out their sphere for them, never urged them to be feminine or jeered at them for being female; who had no axe to grind and no uneasy male dignity to defend; who took them as he found them and was completely unself-conscious. There is no act, no sermon, no parable in the whole Gospel that borrows its pungency from female perversity; nobody could possibly guess from the words and deeds of Jesus that there was anything "funny" about woman's nature."*
> *Dorothy L. Sayers, Are Women Human?*

The starting point for understanding the role of women is the approach of Jesus to women. Dorothy L. Sayers expresses the revolutionary attitude that Jesus displayed. It is difficult for modern western readers of the Bible to grasp His culture-shattering approach. John mentions this explicitly in John 4:27-29:

> *"And at this point His disciples came, and they marveled that. He talked with a woman; yet no one said, "What do You seek?" or, "Why are You talking with her?" The woman then left her water pot, went her way into the city, and said to the men, "Come, see a Man who told me all things that I ever did. Could this be the Messiah?" (John 4:27-29)*

The disciples marvelled that Jesus even spoke with a woman. Jesus' conversation ennobled her because He respected her. It is part of Jesus' love for all sinners that He never spoke down to anyone. Upon the arrival of the disciples the woman fled. The disciples were definitely not yet ready to follow their master in His compassionate handling of this Samaritan woman. It may well have been their looks of amazement and disdain that made her run away. Her message to the people of her city was *"Come see a man."*

The woman of Samaria had been married and divorced five times. She had been through the degradation of being rejected by five men though it would be wrong to assume that the woman had no blame in her failed relationships. Perhaps when she was married she had had dreams of a happy marriage at the first wedding when she may have been as young as sixteen. But by the time we meet her in the gospels she was evasive and tried to hide the fact that she was currently living with a man out of wedlock. The impression is of a woman who was a moral failure without friends or happiness. In a few moments of conversation with Jesus Christ her heart was healed, and joy and wonder returned to her life. She encountered moral purity in the awesome Presence of God in Christ. But most importantly she encountered grace and true manhood. When she said "come see a man" it was the astonished cry of discovering a different kind of man. She became a bearer of glad tidings to the men and women of her city.

When Jesus taught parables and illustrations He frequently made the point of including women. So he told the parable of the Good shepherd seeking the lost sheep, and then the parable of the woman who had lost a coin (Luke 15:1-10). He illustrated his teaching on prayer by describing a man troubling his neighbor (Luke 11:1-11) and then a woman troubling a judge (Luke 18:1-8). He told the parable of the virgins (Matthew 25:1-13) and the parable of the servants given talents (Matthew 25:14-30). He spoke of a woman kneading dough (Matthew 13:33). He had the highest praise for a woman who anointed Him publicly (Luke 7:36-50). Jesus took time to commend Mary for her choice of sitting at His feet (Luke 10:38-42) and He gently and tenderly led Martha to believe in His power to raise the dead (John 11:20-27). No one reading the life of Jesus could ever believe that He thought of women as of secondary importance in His kingdom.

For women to be able to function to the fullest of their gifts and abilities it is necessary that the leading men have this Christ-like attitude. Psalm 68:10 (quoted at the beginning of this section) is a Psalm describing the resurrection and ascension of Jesus. The events surrounding the resurrection are a remarkable fulfilment of this prophecy, especially the fact that the honour of announcing the resurrection to the apostles was given to women. Amazingly the men did not believe them:

> *"It was Mary Magdalene, Joanna, Mary the mother of James, and the other women with them, who told these things to the apostles. And their words seemed to them like idle tales, and they did not believe them."*
> *(Luke 24:10-11)*

Conclusion: Christ's attitude to women is liberating and it is vital that it be the attitude of the Church. Christ sent women with a great message to the apostles and there is no reason to believe that this was merely to be a single event. Christ is still appearing to men and women equally and giving them a message for their generation.

Principle 2 - Men must bear the burden of responsibility.

President Truman had a sign on his desk in the Oval Office:
"The Buck Stops Here!"

There is an inseparable link between responsibility and authority. God has created men and women equal but with different roles. The role of a man is to provide the covering and strength to care for and protect his family. He must bear the final responsibility in the decisions of the home and the Church. He may follow the wisdom of his mother, his wife or his daughter, but he must not shy away from taking responsibility for the decisions he takes. Similarly his mother, wife or daughter must either respect his authority or enfeeble him and deprive him of part of his calling and meaning. A father, husband, son who is not respected is denied one of the core meanings of his life. Women hold great responsibility in politics, business, education and many other walks of life. But in the home they must not take away from the man his leadership and sense of responsibility.

The Church is like the home. It is not a business, and it is not a place of politics. It is a place where men and women function with distinct roles as they do in any home. Paul says of elders that if they cannot rule their home well, then they will be incompetent in the Church:

> *"If a man does not know how to rule his own house, how will he take care of the Church of God?" (1 Timothy 3:5)*

Paul frequently addresses Timothy as his dear son (2 Timothy 2:2) and urges Timothy to relate to others in the Church as family members:

> *"Do not rebuke an older man, but exhort him as a father, younger men as brothers, older women as mothers, younger as sisters, with all purity."*
> *(1 Timothy 5:1-2)*

The Church is God's home and though there may be many other dimensions to the Church, essentially it is His home and "the whole family in heaven and earth is named" after Him as Father. (Ephesians 3:15)

In Christ there is no male or female (Galatians 3:28) but this does not abolish the different roles of male and female in this life in individual families or in the Church. 1 Corinthians 11:1-16 and Ephesians 5:22-33 have no meaning whatsoever if there are no different roles for men and women.

Authority is not a daily issue

> *"A Christian wife's responsibility balances delicately between knowing when to submit and when to outwit. Adapting to our husbands never implies the annihilation of our creativity, rather the blossoming of it."*
> *From "It's my turn" by Ruth Bell Graham.*

In a normal healthy home the question of leadership/responsibility does not arise often. The members of the family go about their business with complete freedom and equality. Authority is not intended to be used to interfere and to dominate in all the areas of family life. Such use of authority would be despotic and abuse the dignity of each family member. The purpose of authority is to liberate each one to exercise choice with a joyous development of their personality.

There are three caveats regarding men bearing authority:

1. Authority is not to be held in a vice like grip as though every issue were some kind of threat. Authority is to be shared and delegated to empower men and women alike. Elders in a Church are to empower people to function freely. Such use of authority is not restricting but is rather liberating.

2. Many elders function with the help and support of their wives. Aquila was probably an elder since a Church met in his home (Romans 16:3-5). On this and two other occasions Priscilla is mentioned before her husband. This must mean that they functioned as a team, and possibly indicates that she was at least as gifted and as active in the ministry as her husband, perhaps more gifted than her husband (why should that be thought at all strange?). It also indicates that Aquila was completely at ease with that arrangement and did not feel it was a threat or a challenge to his authority.

3. The Bible indicates that there are exceptions and in assemblies where there are gifted women the Church should not make the issue of male authority to be like the law of the Medes and Persians. (See my comments earlier in the book examining the implications of the fact that God raised up Deborah pp 66-7).

Leadership becomes an issue during crises

When the home is threatened; whether through dangerous forces that arise to invade and overwhelm it or through poverty and hardship, then the men must rise and protect, laying down their lives to shield each one. At such moments it is right to look to the men to do their job and with courage and fixed determination be the guardians of the family. Men who flee at such moments have denied the very foundation of their significance. An act of cowardice denying responsibility will rob a man of his manhood, and he will only be a shadow of himself after such dereliction of his duty.

Principle 3 - Women may exercise spiritual authority

The Bible teaches that in Christ there is neither male nor female (Galatians 3:28). This applies to the realm of our standing before God. Scripture does not distinguish between male and female when it tells us to resist the devil. Intercession and wrestling with powers and principalities is not limited to men. Many of the greatest intercessors are women.

Illustration from Cameroon:

A dear friend named Vivian Nkwelle was only 13 years old when she came to Christ. She was filled with the Holy Spirit and boldness. It was only a few years after her conversion that she left the city of Nkongsamba to go to a school in a city called Buea some 100 km away. There in class she met another student who was a witch. Vivian boldly witnessed to her and assured her that if she would meet with her the next day God would set her free. Vivian fasted and prayed, then met up with the girl and boldly prayed for the girl and rejoiced to see God honour her faith and her prayers and set the girl free.

****

Illustration from the Revival in the Hebrides:

Peggy and Christine Smith (84 and 82) prayed constantly for revival in their cottage near Barvas village on the Isle of Lewis, the largest of the Hebrides Islands in the bleak northwest of Scotland. God showed Peggy in a dream that revival was coming. Months later, early one winter's morning as the sisters were praying, God gave them an unshakable conviction that revival was near.
Peggy asked her minister James Murray Mackay to call the Church leaders to prayer. Three nights a week the leaders prayed together for months. One night, having begun to pray at 10 p.m., a young deacon from the Free Church read Psalm 24 and challenged everyone to be clean before God. As they waited on God his awesome presence swept over them in the barn at 4 a.m.

When the movement was at its height Peggy sent for the preacher Duncan Campbell, asking him to go to a small, isolated village to hold a meeting. The people of this village did not favour the revival and had already made clear their policy of non-involvement.

Duncan explained the situation to Peggy and told her that he questioned the wisdom of her request. "Besides," he added, "I have no leadings to go to that place." Peggy turned in the direction of his voice (she was blind); her sightless eyes seemed to penetrate his soul. "Mr. Campbell, if you were living as near to God as you ought to be, He would reveal His secrets to you also." Duncan felt like a subordinate being reprimanded for defying his general. He humbly accepted the rebuke as from the Lord, and asked if he and Mr. MacKay could spend the morning in prayer with them. She agreed, and later as they knelt together in the cottage, Peggy prayed:
"Lord, You remember what You told me this morning, that in this village You are going to save seven men who will become pillars in the Church of my fathers. Lord, I have given Your message to Mr. Campbell and it seems he is not prepared to receive it. Oh Lord, give him wisdom, because he badly needs it!"
"All right, Peggy, I'll go to the village," said Duncan when they had finished praying. She replied, "You'd better!" "And God will give you a congregation."

Arriving in the village at seven o'clock they found a large bungalow crowded to capacity with many assembled outside. Duncan gave out his text: "The times of this ignorance God winked at, but now commandeth all men everywhere to repent." When he had finished preaching, a minister beckoned him to the end of the house to speak again to a number of people who were mourning over their sins – among them, Peggy's seven men!

****

Men and women are to wield spiritual authority as they draw close to God. It is fascinating that Duncan Campbell recognized the towering authority of Peggie that came from her close walk with God. The Bible teaches the priesthood of all believers, and all are to draw close to the Holiest of All and there to find that anointing and Presence that clothes us to reign with Jesus as Kings and priests. There should be no sense of hierarchy in the Church. Men and women have different roles in some areas but are completely equal as they serve God in the Spirit and approach His throne.

Leadership is found among men and women

> *Florence Nightingale wanted to be a missionary but there were no opportunities for her. She said, "I would have given the Church my head, my hand, my heart. She would not have them."*

Leadership has to do with many qualities including spiritual authority and gift, a clear vision, a solid walk with God, the ability to organize, the ability to motivate etc.... Many will have no difficulty acknowledging that women have great leadership ability in many different areas such as general ministry (Elizabeth Elliott, Anne Graham-Lotz), Sunday School/ children's ministry and Missionary pioneering (Amy Carmichael, Gladys Aylward, Mary Slessor, Lilias Trotter and Jacky Pullinger) to name but a few.

Deborah:

> *"Some of my best men are women"*
> *General Booth, founder of the Salvation Army.*

The place of Deborah has already been examined earlier in this book but there are some details worth adding. Judges chapter 4 and 5 describe how Deborah ruled Israel for forty years, but there is no suggestion that she broke any spiritual principles of leadership. There are four outstanding aspects of her leadership of Israel:

1. Deborah encouraged the men to take the lead. She exhorted Barak to lead the army into battle. She gave a prophetic word that God had given the enemy into his hand (Judges 4:7). Barak was reluctant to lead whether through unbelief or cowardice and insisted that Deborah go with him to battle (Judges 4:8).

2. Deborah was courageous and willing to go into battle, though she warned that Barak would not enjoy the full honour of victory if she did (Judges 4:9). This was fulfilled when a woman (Jael) struck the final blow (literally).

3. Deborah was full of faith and the calm of believing God's word would be fulfilled (Judges 4:14).

4. Deborah was head and shoulders a better leader than the men who judged Israel. She did not worship idols like Gideon at the end, or fall into sexual temptations like Samson. She was not impulsive like Jephthah, nor cruel and ambitious like Abimelech. Very little is known of her life, but one is left with the impression of a humble, godly woman, walking closely with God.

Many reading this brief account of Deborah's life will conclude that to exclude women from exercising their God given gifts will greatly impoverish the Church. That women may serve the Church is simply foundational to their discipleship. Women serving as deacons is simply a fact of Church life whether it is officially recognized or not (see page 40).

In the chapter on apostles (see page 66) it has already been pointed out that God is able to raise up women to leadership if He so chooses. There are many examples in history where this has happened and has been necessary for various reasons (see page 67).

Principle 4 - Men and women are different and have diverse roles

The difference between the role of men and women lies in the area of final authority. Men are not to misuse their authority and are not to slam the door of opportunity shut, but to provide a safe covering in which both men and women equally may fulfil their ministry.

Once it is understood that there is a difference between men and women designed by the Creator, then it will be realized that this biblical order is established by God for the flourishing of service and not the stifling of it. Men and women working together are in the image of God.

It is at this point that it should be grasped that it is an grievous sin to forbid women to participate freely in open prayer and the gifts of the Spirit. In some Churches women were not allowed to open their mouths in Church services. This is a sin against fifty per cent of God's precious children. In the context of the home this attitude would be unthinkable. This is a misuse of the spiritual home of the Church and presents a distorted image of God, as though women had less value before God than men.

Paul said:

> *"Let your women keep silent in the Churches, for they are not permitted to speak; but they are to be submissive, as the law also says. And if they want to learn something, let them ask their own husbands at home; for it is shameful for women to speak in Church." (1 Corinthians 14:34-35)*

This passage cannot mean that women may never speak in a Church service, as Paul expected them to pray and prophesy (1 Corinthians 11:5). The central issue in 1 Corinthians chapter 14 is the restoration of order in a troubled Church. The Corinthian women were acting in a disruptive manner and were enjoined to maintain silence in the meetings. Few Churches have this specific problem.

What is often overlooked in the same chapter is that people speaking in tongues in a disorderly manner were also enjoined to silence:

> *"If anyone speaks in a tongue, let there be two or at the most three, each in turn, and let one interpret. But if there is no interpreter, let him keep silent in Church, and let him speak to himself and to God."*
> *(1 Corinthians 14 27-28)*

Moreover the same command to keep silence was given to those who prophesied in a disruptive manner speaking over each other, trying to shout each other down:

> *"Let two or three prophets speak, and let the others judge. But if anything is revealed to another who sits by, let the first keep silent."*
> *(1 Corinthians 14:27-30)*

Few if any will believe that the prophets were to keep silence for ever. In the same manner the women can pray and prophesy but must not be unruly in their conduct in the assembly.

Paul said:

> *"Let a woman learn in silence with all submission. And I do not permit*
> *a woman to teach or to have authority over a man, but to be in silence."*
> *(1 Timothy 2:11-12)*

The Greek word for "silence" used by Paul on this occasion is "hesuchia" meaning quietness. (It is the same word in 1 Peter 3:4 where Peter describes the beauty of a "meek and quiet (Greek "hesuchios") spirit. It is a different word than the one used in 1 Corinthians 14:34 "sigao" meaning to be silent. A person may speak "quietly" which is completely different to the concept of being silent. This verse in 1 Timothy is targeting the issue of the usurping of the men in the family of the Church by the women. Paul says that when women disrespect men and try and compete with them for the position of final responsibility then they cross a line which will undermine God's will and order in the family of the Church. The issue here is not whether women may teach or exercise authority, the issue is whether they will persist in doing these things "over the man" i.e. when they undermine the authority of the men and then usurp their place.

It is possible that Paul's strong language is addressing a specific problem that he knew of in Ephesus where Timothy was the pastor. It may be assumed that he would have spoken equally as strongly if a group of men were trying to usurp the authority of the elders. The point is that women must respect authority and so must men. It would be wrong to make from these verses a model of Church governance that excluded the free participation of women in normal Church life.

Some reading these words will find it difficult to accept them because of their cultural and theological background. There are two opposite extremes that shape the minds of many:

1. A World view dominated by men. Most of us come from cultures where women have been repeatedly undervalued. In British society it was less than 100 years ago that women received the right to vote. Today women still receive on average less pay than men in nearly every profession.

2. Materialistic evolution. Evolutionist philosophy denies any fundamental distinction between male and female. According to this world view God did not create the human race and so the distinction between male and female is a product of random processes, not the product of a divine plan.

The problem with our cultural background is that we are not conscious of it or its power to shape our world view. In the same way I, the author of these words, must have the humility to accept that my interpretation is not perfect and may be in need of adjustment and correction. The key is to recognize this. We are all products of our group. We huddle, we imitate, we conform. May God give us grace to think out of the box and to listen to Him and to one another with grace and humility. May we listen to those who hold radically different views to us and not dismiss and despise things we have not heard or considered before.

Biblical world view.

The Bible liberates the women from the endemic culture of male domination. It has a revolutionary message that makes it plain that men and women are equal in the sight of God. But the Bible does not eliminate the difference between the male and the female but rather establishes this difference as the will and plan of the Creator.

Principle 5 - Every Church family is unique

Once this framework is understood it is evident that the structure of the Church is not a template that must be legalistically reproduced in every situation. Just as families vary enormously; so too each local Church is unique. A Church which has some very gifted and able women will do well to provide opportunity for them to flourish in their ministry, but equally this will require mature men who are secure in themselves and do not feel threatened by the strength of the women.

If the five principles described above are fully embraced then the members in each locality will be able to work out their relationships. Imitation of others, or criticism of others is unhelpful. Just as each husband and wife relationship is unique so too each assembly will have an inimitable pattern and shape.

Conclusion: Applying the principles.

These principles provide answers to our questions.

Q: Can women preach, teach and exercise public ministry?

A: The Bible reveals that men are to bear the burden of leadership in the Church. Women may freely function in that context. Women may engage in all public ministry as long as they do not cross the line of usurping authority. Then it is for the local elders to decide.

It is fascinating to notice that some are strongly opposed to women teaching and preaching but will gladly read books such as the following: Steams in the Desert by Mrs. Cowman, War on the Saints by Jesse Penn Lewis, many titles by Amy Carmichael. Hymns by women are also popular such as *"Blessed Assurance"* by Fanny Crosby, or *"Just as I am"* by Frances Ridley Havergal

.

Q: What about Churches where there are no men?

A: No woman can be accused of undermining men if there are none present.

Q: What about Churches where all the men are new converts?

A: It is obviously right for women to lead in such a situation. But wisdom and humility will be required on the part of both the men and the women. Watchman Nee was converted through the preaching of a Chinese evangelist named Dora Yu. He was taught the Bible by some women in his early years (paradoxically by Missionary Margaret Barber who had informal ties with the Plymouth brethren in which traditionally only men are allowed to speak!) As he matured so their relationship changed. However some converts never mature to the level of leading an assembly.

Conclusion:

The Bible is not the source of male chauvinism rather it is the foundation for the liberation of women. Men and women have different roles but there is a freedom in the love of Christ that brings out the magnificent plan of the Creator for both male and female. God reveals Himself through both working together in that harmony and unity that is found so uniquely in the Church the body of Christ. The Church is a company of people in heaven and on earth gathered around the throne of God in worship and love for Father, Son and Holy Spirit. The voices of men and women blend in worship and service of their Redeemer. May each member of that wonderful multitude realise the fullness of Christ in this life so that He may be abundantly glorified.

Study Guide.

This study guide can be used in a variety of contexts – from personal study, house groups, to Bible studies and leadership training. The different sections relate directly to the chapters and are linked by page numbers where relevant. Use them in their entirety or select a few questions for discussion or study.

THE EMPEROR AND THE HEIR

1. What does this story teach us about some of the most important characteristics of leaders? How did Lee Wang show a) courage b) lack of hypocrisy c) honesty
2. When Solomon became King of Israel (1 Kings 3:4-14) he pleased God by his requests. Read his prayer and discuss what it was that made him a good leader.
3. Look at John 13 when Jesus washed His disciples' feet and reflect on the teaching of Jesus and the reaction of His disciples.
4. Why is good leadership so important to the health of Churches?
5. What is the heart of leadership?
6. In what way is leadership something that concerns the whole Church?

PART I ~ THE SPIRITUAL LIFE OF LEADERS

CHAPTER 1 - THE ENTHRONING OF CHRIST.

1. How would you lead someone to surrender themselves to Jesus Christ? (9)
2. How is the administration of the kingdom of God so different to that of an earthly kingdom? (8,9)
3. Why is the place of surrender to God so holy? (9,10)
4. Why is it that many will find the baptism of the Spirit in the place of surrender?
5. What are some of the practical signs that we are living a life of surrender to Jesus? (10)
6. What role does waiting on God have in making Jesus Christ Lord of our lives? (11)
7. What is the main enemy of waiting on God?
8. Which is more important in learning to listen to God: meditation or self-denial? (12)
9. What are the benefits that we gain from learning to wait on God? (12,13)
10. Why must we persevere and learn to wait longer in God's presence? (14,15)
11. What was Paul so passionately seeking in Philippians 3:7-11?
12. What are the snares of becoming absorbed with the ministry?
13. "If a man dethrone God he always makes himself God. If God does not occupy the throne of every life then man will assume for Himself the very functions of Deity." (G. Campbell Morgan, Acts of the Apostles, p. 233) Do you agree with Campbell Morgan? (15)
14. Why is serving God not contradictory to serving people?
15. "The person who prays will go out to seek the lost, and the person who goes out to seek the lost will often be on his knees praying." Is this always true? (16)
16. What would be the mark of a person who idolises prayer?
17. Why does God sometimes withdraw Himself for a season?

CHAPTER 2 – THE CALL OF MOSES

1. In what way can Moses be described as a servant leader? How is this also true of Jesus? In what way does the verse in Mark 10:45 sum up this truth? "For even the Son of Man did not come to be served, but to serve, and to give His life a ransom for many." (Mark 10:45) (18)
2. What is the primary call of God in Mark 3:13-15? (19)
3. What can parents learn from the story of Moses and the role of his parents in his life? (22)
4. Why is Moses' repentance such a great leap of faith? Can you think of any examples from people you know or from history who have also given up much to serve God?
5. What would Moses' life have been like if he had not repented? (23)
6. "There must be great renunciations if there are to be great Christian careers." Do you agree with James Denny? (25)
7. What were the hard lessons Moses had to learn before God could use him? How would this affect his teaching of God's people? (26,27)
8. What are the three main lessons for life that we learn from the temptations of Moses and Jesus in the wilderness?
9. What does the burning bush symbolise? (28)
10. Why did Moses not react more eagerly to the call of God to go and deliver the people from Egypt? (29)
11. What is the meaning of God's name Yahweh? (30,31)
12. How do some people treat God like a dentist?
13. How do weaknesses such as Moses' speech defect glorify God? (33)
14. What do we learn from the fact that God had an objection to Moses? (34)
15. What are the great lessons we can learn from Moses and how can we apply them to our lives?

CHAPTER 3 - PAUL'S TEACHING ON LEADERSHIP

1. What are the implications of being a slave of Jesus Christ? (37)
2. Do you agree that women can be servants or deacons in the Church? (39,40)
3. Under rowers were also slaves, so what special insights do we learn from this word? (40,41)
4. Think of a practical example of how a leader might be a steward of God's goods.
5. What are the three things that an overseer is watching over?
6. What do you learn from the word "elder" meaning literally an older man? (42,43)
7. In what way are all Christians and especially leaders soldiers of Christ? (44)
8. What are the lessons we can take from the metaphor that leaders are: (44-49)
   a. Soldiers
   b. Shepherds.
   c. Farmers.
   d. Athletes.
9. What lessons do you glean from the story of George Whitefield? (51)
10. Is it right for pastors to be supported by the Churches they serve? (50)
11. Why did Paul refuse to exercise this right?
12. How does the love of money destroy people in general and ministers in particular? Can you think of a verse from the lips of Jesus that warns about the danger of money? (52)
13. What was the sin of Balaam? (53)
14. What was the sin of Judas? (54,55)
15. What does a leader's attitude to other ministries show about his character? (55,56)
16. What is the teaching of Paul on suffering? (56,57)
17. How does Paul relate the power of his ministry to suffering?

PART II ~ APOSTLES AND SPIRITUAL LEADERSHIP

CHAPTER 4 – APOSTLES: A PATTERN FOR LEADERSHIP

1. What is an apostle? (62)
2. Do you think there are apostles today?
3. Why is it important for all Christians to understand something of the apostolic ministry? (63)
4. Do you agree that God can raise up women to positions of leadership? (65,66)
5. Why should all Christians aspire to some measure of leadership? (67,68)
6. What are the two words most frequently used to describe Christians in the New Testament? (68)
7. Why are titles of secondary importance? What function do they serve? (68, 69)
8. What is the difference between elders and the five ministries of apostles, prophets, evangelists, pastors and teachers.
9. What is the right attitude of believers if there are problems in the leadership of a Church? What would be the wrong attitude? (71)
10. In what way are Leaders/apostles on display? (71,72)
11. What do we learn from the fact that the apostles were probably all young men? (72,73)
12. Why is it a great comfort that God uses imperfect men and women? (74)
13. Why did Jesus choose Judas? (75,76)
14. What is the central call of leaders? (76,77)
15. In what way does Jesus embody all the prophets and men of faith of the Old Testament? (78,79)
16. What are the implications of affirming that Jesus is the Messiah? (80,81)

CHAPTER 5 – APOSTLES AND REVELATION

1. What did Jesus come to reveal about God that we could not know any other way? (82)
2. Why does the revelation of who Jesus is change our lives?
3. What is the essential message of Jesus in:
    a. The sermon on the Mount?
    b. The parables of the kingdom?
    c. The parable of the prodigal son?   (85,86)
4. What was the cumulative effect of being present at all the amazing miracles that Jesus did? (87)
5. What were the characteristics of Jesus that shine through the gospel accounts? (87,88)
6. What does the raising of Jairus's daughter (Mark 5:21-43) teach about Jesus? (88,89)
7. What does the Transfiguration (Mark 9:2-10) teach us about Jesus? (89,90)
8. What does Gethsemane (Mark 14:32-42) teach us about the heart of God? (91,92)
9. What are the implications of the crucifixion of Jesus once we realise that He is God in human form? (92)

CHAPTER 6 – APOSTLES AND BROKENNESS

1. Why is it vital that ministers do not become obsessed with power? (95)
2. Why did Jesus need to show the disciples that they were afraid of death? Consider the example of John Wesley. How did his experience lead him to a deeper experience of God? (96)
3. What does Jesus attitude to children in Mark 10:13-14 teach us about kingdom values? (97)
4. Why is it important for a leader to be able to admit being wrong?
5. Read Mark 9:33-4. What is the characteristic of leaders that might cause them to be competitive? (98,99)
6. The apostles found it hard to pray with Jesus. Why is honesty so important when facing spiritual challenge? (99)
7. Can you explain why Peter cried out "I am a sinful man!" in Luke 5:8? (101)
8. How do you explain that Jesus could rebuke Peter and say that it he was identified with Satan? How do you define the word "Satanic"? (103)
9. What was the cause of Peter's deepest brokenness? Why do we all need to touch such depths if we are to be faithful leaders?
10. If our commitment is not the foundation of the Christian life, what is? (106)
11. What healed and restored Peter to hope? (105)
12. What are the qualities that made Peter such a great man of God?
13. Why is brokenness a key for the power of the Holy Spirit to be released in us? (106)
14. Do you agree that the training of the 12 apostles was one of the greatest achievements of Jesus' ministry? Explain. (106)

CHAPTER 7 – APOSTLES: WITNESSES OF THE CROSS

1. Why is the cross foolishness to the natural man? (108)
2. What did the Centurion understand by watching Jesus die?
3. What were the essential elements of the exchange between Jesus and the murderer who died beside Jesus? Think how this would give you understanding about how to lead a person to Christ even on their death bed. (109)
4. Why were nearly all the apostles absent as Jesus died? (109)
5. What does John 3:16 teach us about Jesus personal knowledge of the cross three years before His death? (111)
6. What was the role of the Father in the drama of the cross?
7. What did the Holy Spirit see that was hidden from the onlookers as Jesus died? (113)
8. When did the apostles become the first witnesses of the cross as God sees it? (113)
9. Do you think that believers today can discover the same freshness and power of the cross as the apostles? Explain. (114)
10. What are the six great truths about the cross that can be found in the writings of Paul and the book of Hebrews? (115)
11. Why is the link between the Holy Spirit and the cross such an important foundation for spiritual leadership? (116)

CHAPTER 8 – APOSTLES: MINISTERS OF THE HOLY SPIRIT

1. What did Jesus teach about the kingdom of God in John 13? Why is this a preparation for His teaching about the Holy Spirit? (117)
2. When did God create a community of love? (118)
3. What is the key work of the Holy Spirit in salvation? (119)
4. What is the deeper knowledge of indwelling that comes through the baptism with the Holy Spirit? (120)
5. Why is this so important if we are to learn to abide in Christ?
6. The Holy Spirit produces a close relationship with Jesus in prayer. Can you think of other verses that teach about prayer in and through the Holy Spirit? (122)
7. What are the greater works that believers do after the coming of the Holy Spirit? (122)
8. If the Holy Spirit teaches and guides us why do we still need Bible teachers and pastors? (123)
9. The Holy Spirit makes believers to be effective witnesses of Jesus. How does this work? (124)
10. "He (the Holy Spirit) will convict the world of sin, righteousness and judgment." Why is this so important if we are to lead sinners to salvation? (125,126)
11. Why is loving Jesus the greatest condition for receiving the Holy Spirit? (127)
12. Peter and the 120 in the upper room waited for the Holy Spirit to come on them. Does this mean we also have to wait for Him to come on us? (127,128)
13. What do you believe are the main signs that we have received the Holy Spirit? (129)
14. What do you learn about the work of the Holy Spirit from the events in Samaria and Caesarea? Why is apostolic input so vital in outpourings of the Holy Spirit? (132)
15. What will happen if the ministry of the Spirit is lost? (136)

PART III ~ PRACTICAL CONSIDERATIONS

CHAPTER 9 – MANAGING CHANGE

1. Do you think we live in an age of accelerated change? Explain and give examples. (139,140)
2. There are two kinds of conflict afflicting the Church today: superficial areas of culture, and more serious areas of morality and Bible interpretation. Give examples of both. (140)
3. How did Jesus challenge the culture of His day? (139-140)
4. Why is leadership the management of change? (140)
5. What are the main elements of the world view of the 21st century? (141)
6. Why must the Church not be shaped by this view? How does the Christian Church differ from it? (142)
7. How can we reach the unchurched "Y" generation? (143,144)
8. Why is it so important for us to hold fast to the Bible if we are to reach a world subject to constant change? (144,145)
9. Would you add anything to the list of vital areas of eternal truth that are the foundation of our Christian faith? (147)
10. "I have become all things to all men" (I Corinthians 9:22) What was the reason that made Paul willing to give up his personal preferences? (148)
11. Why might we have to eat pork (metaphorically) if we want to reach the lost? (149,150)
12. Why are God's standards of sexuality morality so absolute? What will happen to the society that has no moral standards?
13. How would you describe a Christian with a "free spirit"? What would be the qualities of a person who is the exact opposite?
14. Finney describes how a revival was stopped due to a conflict between Christians on the subject of baptism. Do you agree with Finney? Does this change your attitude to other Christians of other denominations? (153)
15. Why is the Day of Judgment the final absolute that we must never lose from view? (153)

CHAPTER 10 – ACCOUNTABILITY

1. Make a list of things for which we will give account when we stand before Jesus at His coming? (155)

2. Why is it important that believers fear God? Have you a strong view on whether believers can lose their salvation? Can you think of scriptures that help you understand the Bible's teaching on this subject? (156)

3. Summarise the three reasons why accountability is important for ministers in this present life. (157)

4. While structures may be useful, what is the most important quality in a person who will help us to give some account of ourselves? (159)

5. Describe the kind of friend we need. (159)

6. Why is accountability best within an eldership? (160)

7. Give biblical examples of accountability through fathers in the faith. (167)

8. Are we accountable to the Church? (161)

9. What steps could we take to make accountability a part of our life and ministry? (162,163)

10. What are the snares of the ministry that can be avoided through accountability? (discuss)

11. What are the positive benefits of accountability? (164)

12. Why is it important for ministers to think about succession early in their ministry? (164,165)

13. Reflect on the principles of success. Does any stand out as being more important to you personally? Are there any steps you need to take to improve your walk with God? (165,166)

14. From the examples of accountability in the New Testament what are the most important lessons? (167,168)

15. Accountability in Moral behaviour: why is it so important for ministers of the gospel more than any other group of people? (169)

CHAPTER 11 – THE PREACHING MINISTRY

1. What are the essential foundations of the preaching ministry? Place them in the order of importance that you believe to be correct. (174 – 180)
2. What strikes you about the testimony of D.L. Moody? (174)
3. To what degree is the messenger himself the message? (175)
4. What is more important, our call to serve God or to serve people? How do these two aspects of ministry sometimes conflict with one another? (180)
5. What is the main message that preachers must never forget? (180)
6. What are the three great snares of the preaching ministry? (182 – 184)
7. Can you think of any ways in which congregations can help their ministers to overcome temptation? (discuss)
8. What do you learn from the testimony of Spurgeon's conversion? (185)
9. What can we practically do to increase our effectiveness in ministry? (185 – 188)
10. Review the practical keys to preaching and discuss which are the most important. (189 – 193)
11. Can you think of anything that might be added to this list?
12. What is the high goal of the preaching ministry? (193)

CHAPTER 12 – THE ROLE OF WOMEN

1. What are the difficulties of making generalizations about the role of women? (194)

2. How do we know that God wants both men and women to be fully active in the life and ministry of the Church? Point to passages of scripture to support this. (195)

3. Make a list of women that God used to speak to Israel in the Bible. (195) Why do you think that it was given to women to announce the Resurrection of Jesus? (198)

4. How would you summarise the attitude of Christ to women? (196 – 198)

5. Do you agree that men must bear the burden of responsibility? Give Bible references to support your view.

6. Can women exercise spiritual authority? (202 – 205)

7. What are the main differences in the roles of men and women? (206 – 209)

8. Do you agree that every Church family is unique? Reflect on Churches in the New Testament. (209 - 210)

9. Deborah is a rare example of a woman in leadership in the Bible. What were her outstanding qualities? Why is it so important to understand this Bible character to help us understand the role of women? (205)

10. What did Paul mean when he urged women to be silent in the Church in 1 Corinthians 14:34-35? Were others also to be silent? (207)

11. What was the Greek word used by Paul in 1 Timothy 2:11-12. What do you think is the main problem that Paul was writing about in this verse? (208)

12. What are the main elements of the biblical world view in respect to men and women? How does this conflict with the world's view? (209)

To access further study materials and books by this author please visit www.leswheeldon.com

The following books are available on Amazon:

Take Me to Your Leader: Rediscovering the Heart of Spiritual Leadership

Hearing God's Heart: a Daily Devotional

The Christian's Compass: A resource of Biblical Beliefs

Blessed or Cursed: A Study of Galatians

Index

Made in the USA
Charleston, SC
04 February 2016